THE Holocaust

THE Holocaust

Editor
Geoffrey Wigoder

A
Grolier Student
Library

Volume 1
Abwehr to Extermination Camps

Grolier Educational

SHERMAN TURNPIKE, DANBURY, CONNECTICUT

Concept, Content and Editorial Advisor
Charles E. Smith

Managing Editor
Rachel Gilon

Library of Congress Cataloging-in-Publication Data

The Holocaust.
    p.   cm.
  Summary. Articles identify and describe individuals and events
connected with the persecution of Jews and others across Europe in
the 1930s and 1940s.
  ISBN 0-7172-7637-6
  1. Holocaust, Jewish (1939-1945)—Encyclopedias, Juvenile.
[1. Holocaust, Jewish (1939-1945)—Encyclopedias.]
D804.25.H65   1996
940.53'18'03—dc20

                       96-9566
                          CIP
                          AC

Published 1997 by Grolier Educational,
Sherman Turnpike, Danbury, Connecticut
© 1997 by Charles E. Smith Books, Inc.
Second Printing 1999
Third Printing 2002

Set ISBN 0-7172-7637-6
Volume 1: ISBN 0-7172-7638-4

For information, address the publisher:
Grolier Educational, Sherman Turnpike, Danbury, Connecticut 06816

Cover design by Smart Graphics
Planned and produced by The Jerusalem Publishing House, Jerusalem
Printed in Hong Kong

contributors

HAIM AVNI, Ph.D., Institute of Contemporary Jewry, The Hebrew University of Jerusalem

ARYEH BARNEA, Principal, The Denmark Comprehensive High School, Jerusalem

VICTORIA BARNETT, Church Relations, United States Holocaust Memorial Museum, Washington D.C.

TAMARA BEKEFI, Living Testimonies Holocaust Project, Montreal, Quebec

MICHAEL BERENBAUM, Ph.D., Director, United States Holocaust Research Institute, United States Holocaust Memorial Museum, Washington D.C.

ELIZABETH BERMAN, Director, U.S. Holocaust Research Institute, United States Holocaust Memorial Museum, Washington D.C.

MICHAEL BLACHER, Los Angeles, CA

MICHAEL BRENNER, Ph.D., Tauber Institute for the Study of European Jewry, Brandeis University, Waltham, MA

DONALD BLOXHAM, Ph.D., Dept. of History, University of Southampton

ARIEH DOOBOV, Associate Editor, Institute of the World Jewish Congress, Jerusalem

ABRAHAM J. EDELHEIT, Ph.D., Dept. of History, Kingsborough Community College, City University of New York

ELIZABETH EPPLER, Ph.D., Former Director, Institute of Jewish Affairs, London

MICHELLE FELLNER, Writer, Jerusalem

JOSEY FISHER, Director, Holocaust Oral History

Archive Gratz College, Melrose Park, PA

ZEV GARBER, Ph.D., Dept. of Jewish Studies, Los Angeles Valley College, Los Angeles, CA

NEIL GREGOR, Ph.D., Dept. of History, University of Southampton

JOSHUA GREY, Publication Dept., United States Holocaust Memorial Museum, Washington D.C.

MICAH HALPERN, Historian and Lecturer, Jerusalem

PATRICIA HEBERER, Research Historian, United States Holocaust Memorial Museum, Washington D.C.

HILMAR HOFFMAN, Ph.D., President of the Goethe-Institute, Munich

SANDRA KAISER, Historical Editor, United States Holocaust Memorial Museum, Washington D.C.

SERGE KLARSFELD, Paris

KONRAD KWIET, Deputy Director, Center for Comparative Genocide Studies, University of Macquarie, Australia

NATASHA LEHRER, CD Rom Producer, Jerusalem

DOV LEVIN, Historian, Institute of Contemporary Jewry, The Hebrew University of Jerusalem

DVORA LEWY, Picture Researcher

DEBORAH LIPSTADT, Department of Religion, Emory University, Atlanta, GA

ZIVA AMISHAI-MAISELS, Dept. of Art History, The Hebrew University of Jerusalem

JÜGEN MATTHÄUS, Historian, War Crimes Prosecution Support Unit, Australia

MICHELLE MAZEL, Writer and Journalist, Jerusalem

DAN MICHMAN, Dept. of Jewish History, Bar Ilan University, Ramat Gan

SCOTT MILLER, University Programs Coordinator, United States Holocaust Research Institute, Washington D.C.

ANNE·MOLINEU, Research Historian, United States Holocaust Memorial Museum, Washington, D.C.

JOANNA NEWMAN, Dept. of History, University of Southampton

EDWARD PHILLIPS, Research Historian, United States Holocaust Memorial Museum, Washington, D.C.

JO REILLY, Ph.D., Education and Outreach Officer, Institute of Contemporary History and Wiener Library, London

KEVIN ROSEN, The Hebrew University of Jerusalem

ALEX ROSSINO, Research Historian, United States Holocaust Memorial Museum, Washington, D.C.

BARBARA P. SUTNICK M.A., Educational Editor, Jewish Education, Jerusalem

REUVEN DAVID SUTNICK, M.A., Rabbinic Literature, Jerusalem

ABRAHAM I SHAFIR, Ph.D., Bible Department & Chairman Head of Junior High School Track Studies, Giv'at Washington College

CHARLES E. SMITH, Charles E. Smith Books, Freehold, NJ

KENNETH STERN, American Jewish Committee, New York, N.Y.

DEREK SYMER, Research Historian, United States Holocaust Memorial Museum, Washington, D.C.

HILLEL TRYSTER, Deputy Director and Researcher, Steven Spielberg Jewish Film Archive, The Hebrew University of Jerusalem

MARTIN VAN CREVELD, Ph.D., Dept. of History, The Hebrew University of Jerusalem

LAURENCE WEINBAUM, Ph.D., Senior Research and Editorial Officer, World Jewish Congress, Jerusalem

BRET WERB, Musicologist, United States Holocaust Memorial Museum, Washington, D.C.

GEOFFREY WIGODER Ph.D., Director of Oral History Department, Institute of Contemporary Jewry, The Hebrew University of Jeruslaem

DANNY WOOL, Writer, Jerusalem

CAROL ZAWATSKY, Assistant Director, Community Programs, United States Holocaust Memorial Museum, Washington, D.C.

BIBLIOGRAPHY: LINDA VERTREES, Division Head, Acquisitions Division, The Chicago Public Library, Chicago, IL.

INDEX: SHLOMO KETKO, Translator, Language Editor, Jerusalem

introduction

Cruel periods have occurred all too often in history and in all parts of the world, but none of these was more shocking than what is known as the Holocaust—the deliberate humiliation and murder of 6 million Jews in Europe by the Nazis and their collaborators in many countries during World War II (1939–1945). Never before has such a systematic attempt been made to wipe an entire people off the face of the earth. The Nazis even checked up on origins so that half-Jews could also be destroyed and no trace of "Jewish blood" be left. And this horror occurred at the very center of what we call the "civilized world."

The Jews are one of the world's oldest people. The Bible is the source of information on their original religious and moral message, which so greatly influenced humankind. Their homeland was Israel, but from an early period there were Jewish communities in other countries. Their religion separated them from their pagan neighbors. Later, even Christianity and Islam, which had strong Jewish roots, isolated and persecuted them. The dislike of the Jews came to be called antisemitism.

Antisemitism had many roots, but up to the 19th century, it was mainly religiously based. But then, in the 19th century, new forms of antisemitism appeared. One of these was based on the belief that humankind is made up of different races—some of which were naturally superior and some lower. In the 20th century, this theory attracted a growing number of followers. One of these was Adolf Hitler, who, together with his followers, believed that the Germans belonged to a race of supermen—the Aryans. All other people were inferior and meant to serve them. One people in particular, they decided, were the lowest of all races and should be wiped out. These were the Jews.

When Hitler and the Nazis came to power in Germany (1933), they could put their theories into practice. They removed Jews from the rest of German society. As the Germans took over other countries in Europe, they did the same there. In 1939, Hitler attacked Poland, thereby starting World War II, and within a couple of years, was master of nearly all Europe. This meant that over half the world's 17 million Jews were now under his control. Within less than five years, he had killed the great majority of them, in various terrible ways.

There were also other groups who were the victims of the Nazis. These included the disabled, the Gypsies, communists, Soviet Russian prisoners of war, homosexuals, and political prisoners. They too were subject to persecution and merciless killing.

But the Holocaust is not only a tale of horror. It has its aspects of inspiration and courage. Among the Jews, there was the determination to maintain a human face despite the attempts to turn them into animals. This included spiritual resistance, by which they continued with their education and traditions under impossible circumstances, as well as the acts of physical resistance, despite the overwhelming nature of the German forces. And there is the story of the many non-Jews who were shocked at the plight of the Jews and took steps to save them, at the risk of their own lives.

These volumes cover every aspect: the general historical background; biographies of the Nazi leaders; the fate of the Jews country by country, ghetto by ghetto, camp by camp; the assistance—or its absence—of countries that were not under German occupation; the bravery of non-Jews who tried to rescue Jews; and the outcome of the war, with its trials of Nazi criminals and the desperate search of Jewish survivors for a new home. The entries have been written by scholars from many countries, to whom we express our appreciation, especially to Dr. Michael Berenbaum, Director of the Holocaust Research Institute in the United States Holocaust Museum in Washington, D.C.

The history of the Holocaust is now taught in many schools, not only because of its historic importance, but for its universal message. Ordinary people can very easily become savage barbarians if they do not fully realize what the results of prejudice, racism, and hate can be. Indeed, many ordinary people in Europe were sucked into the events of the Holocaust and became accomplices of the killers.

Still today, there are antisemites who try to say that the story of the Holocaust is exaggerated, or even that it never happened! It is, therefore, vital to study the Holocaust. It is no accident that the central Holocaust museum of the United States should have been built right in the center of the nation's capital—on Washington's Mall. The Holocaust is not a distant event that happened in a far-away place; its significance is for all of us. By our knowledge of what happened then, we become alerted to the awareness that such a tragedy should never happen again—to anyone.

HOW TO USE

The entries are in alphabetical order. Cross references are indicated in the text by words appearing in small capitals (like NAZI PARTY) which refer to related entries.

At the beginning of the volume 1 is a Glossary. This contains a list and explanations of the more unusual and technical terms related to the Holocaust and to the Nazi regime. The reader who finds a difficult word in the text should turn to the glossary for an explanation.

Boxes, often to be found within the entries, give quotations or stories or further information connected to the entry.

At the end of each volume appears an index for that volume. An index covering the entire work appears at the end of Volume 4.

glossary

ABWEHR Intelligence service of German army.

AKTION Military operation. Operation against Jews, especially in ghettos for purposes of deportation.

ALIYA Immigration of Jews to Palestine (Israel). Aliya Bet see "Illegal Immigration."

ALLIES, ALLIED POWERS Alliance of countries fighting Nazi Germany in World War II, primarily Britain, France, Soviet Russia, United States.

ALTESTENRAT, Literally Council of Elders. Another name for Judenrat (see below).

ANSCHLUSS The German annexation of Austria in 1938.

ARMÉE JUIVE (Jewish Army) French Zionist resistance movement.

ARROW CROSS Hungarian anti-Semitic party.

ARYAN A broad division of the human race. Germans identified themselves with the Aryans whom they called a master race. The Jews were seen as "Non-Aryan" and inferior. The parts of a city outside the Jewish ghetto were called the Aryan side.

ARYANIZATION The forced takeover of Jewish businesses and properties by the Germans.

AUSCHWITZ Death camp in Poland (Polish name, Oswiecim). Apart from the original camp, there was an extermination center at nearby Birkenau (Auschwitz II) and a slave labor camp at nearby Buna-Monowitz (Auschwitz III).

AXIS The alliance of Germany, Italy and Japan in World War II.

BADGE Distinguishing mark which had to be worn by Jews under Nazi rule. It usually took the form of a yellow star of David stitched onto an outer garment.

BALKANS The countries of south east Europe.

BALTIC STATES Three states (Lithuania, Latvia, Estonia) adjoining the Baltic Sea in north east Europe.

BARBAROSSA Code name for the German invasion of Soviet Russia which started on 22 June 1941.

BEER-HALL PUTSCH An attempt by Hitler and his associates in Munich to take over the Bavarian government on 9 November 1923. It failed and Hitler was imprisoned.

BERIHA Flight of Holocaust survivors from eastern Europe toward Palestine (Israel) in the years 1944-1948.

BLITZKREIG A lightning war.

BLOOD LIBEL (or Ritual Murder Libel) False antisemitic allegation that Jews kill non-Jews and use their blood to make their Passover bread.

BOHEMIA AND MORAVIA Part of Czechoslovakia which was under German control (a protectorate) during the War World II.

BOLSHEVISM The communist regime that took over Russia in October/November 1917.

BUND Jewish socialist party, active especially in eastern Europe.

COLD WAR State of enmity without actual war that emerged between the United States and Soviet Russia in the post-war world.

COLLABORATOR Non-German who worked with the Nazi invaders of his/her country.

CREMATORIUM Installation for burning bodies.

D-DAY The day (6 June 1944) the western allies landed in France to open a Second Front (the first being fought by the Russians in the east) against the Russians.

DEATH CAMP Camp established by the Nazis for purposes of mass killing of prisoners sent there.

DIASPORA Jews living outside Palestine (Israel).

DISPLACED PERSON (DP) Person driven out of his home during the war; after the war, Holocaust survivor who could or would not go back to his original place of residence.

EINSATZGRUPPE Mobile killing squads who moved along behind the German army with the object of mass-killing those whom the Nazis regarded as their enemies (especially the Jews). They had sub-units called Einsatzkommando.

EXTERMINATION Complete destruction. The Nazis planned the "extermination" (or liquidation) of the Jews.

FASCISM Italian nationalist movement founded by Benito Mussolini. A member of the movement was called a fascist.

"FINAL SOLUTION" Nazi code word for the extermination of the Jews.

FÜHRER German for "leader." Adolf Hitler's title.

GAULEITER Nazi party head of a Gau, which was a territorial unit.

GENDARMERIE Local police.

GENERALGOUVERNEMENT (General Government) That part of Poland which was not absorbed into Germany. It was ruled by a German governor.

GESTAPO The Nazi secret police.

GHETTO Part of a town in which Jews were confined.

GOVERNMENT-IN-EXILE Government established outside their territories by countries overrun by the Germans.

HEBREW The ancient language of the Jewish people.

HITLER YOUTH Organization for Nazi boys.

HLINKA GUARD Militia of the People's Party in Slovakia.

HOLOCAUST The persecution and systematic destruction of the Jewish people by the Nazis. In Hebrew, Shoah.

INTERNATIONAL MILITARY TRIBUNAL Court established by the Allies (United States, Great Britain, Soviet Russia, and France) after the war to try Nazi criminals.

IRON GUARD The fascist movement in Romania.

JUDENFREI (or Judenrein) German term meaning "free of Jews" for place and area in which Jews no longer live.

JUDENRAT (Jewish Council) Council of Jews appointed by the Nazis to govern the Jewish population, especially in ghettos, under German orders.

KAPO Supervisor of labor in camps, often chosen from among the Jewish prisoners.

KRISTALLNACHT ("night of the broken glass") Organized attack on Jews in Germany and Austria on 9 and 10 November 1938 in which Jewish stores were smashed and looted, synagogues burned down, and many Jews sent to concentration camps.

LABOR CAMPS Camps in which the prisoners were forced to work under inhuman conditions.

LEBENSRAUM (living space) Term used for the Nazis for areas they sought to conquer, especially in eastern Europe, to expand German territory.

LIQUIDATION see Extermination.

LUFTWAFFE German air force.

MAQUIS French resistance movement.

MEIN KAMPF ("My Struggle") Book written by Adolf Hitler expounding Nazi ideology (published 1925-1926).

MISCHLINGE Term used by Nazis for people with one or two Jewish grandparents.

MUNICH PUTSCH see Beer Hall Putsch.

MUSELMANN Concentration camp inmate so thin he or she has become like a skeleton and is close to death.

NATIONALISM Movement aimed at strengthening national feeling.

NATIONAL SOCIALISM (National Socialist Party) German national movement led by Adolf Hitler. The term was shortened to Nazism and its adherents were called Nazis.

NAZIS see National Socialism.

NAZI-SOVIET PACT Agreement between Nazi Germany and Soviet Russia, 19-23 August 1939, which opened the way for the German invasion of Poland.

NIGHT OF THE LONG KNIVES Night (30 June-1 July) when the SS massacred leaders of the SA.

NUMERUS CLAUSUS Restriction of number of Jews allowed in a university.

NUREMBERG TRIAL Trial of Nazi leaders after the war (1945-1946).

ORGANIZATION TODT Nazi organization for large scale construction based on the use of forced labor.

OSTLAND Regions of eastern Europe occupied by the Germans.

PALESTINE Country in Middle East which during the war years was governed by the British. Its inhabitants are Jews and Arabs. In 1948, part of Palestine became the Jewish state of Israel.

PARTISANS Groups of resistance fighters.

POGROM Attack on Jews.

QUISLING A traitor.

RAZZIA A roundup of Jews.

RED ARMY The army of Soviet Russia.

REICHSTAG The German parliament.

"RIGHTEOUS AMONG THE NATIONS" Title given by the Israel Holocaust Memorial Institution, Yad Vashem, to non-Jews who risked their lives to rescue Jews during the Holocaust.

RITUAL MURDER LIBEL see Blood Libel.

RSHA Head office of Nazi security and intelligence services.

SA Nazi storm troopers used to undermine the Weimar Republic and ensure Hitler's rise to power.

SD The security and intelligence service of the SS.

SELEKTION (Selekzia) Selection by Nazis in ghettos of Jews for deportation; and selection in camps of those who were to be put to death immediately, and those who were to be sent to forced labor.

SEPHARDIM Jews originating from Spain and Portugal.

SHOAH Hebrew for Holocaust.

SLOVAKIA Part of Czechoslovakia which was independent during World War II.

SONDERKOMMANDO Unit of SS or Einsatzgruppe; also unit of Jews selected by Nazis in death camps to dispose of corpses.

SOVIET UNION (Soviet Russia) The communist state of Russia.

SPANISH CIVIL WAR War in Spain, 1936-1939, when rebels led by General Francisco Franco attacked the elected government and eventually came to power—with the assistance of Nazi Germany and Fascist Italy.

SS Nazi party police and the main instrument of Nazi terror.

SWASTIKA Ancient symbol adopted by the Nazis as their emblem.

THIRD REICH The Nazi regime in Germany, 1933-1945.

TRANSNISTRIA Province in southern Ukraine occupied by Romania, 1914-1944.

UMSCHLAGPLATZ Gathering-place in Warsaw for Jews about to be deported to death camps.

UNITED NATIONS RELIEF AND RE-HABILITATION ADMINISTRATION

(UNRAA) Organization founded by the United Nations in 1943 to help victims of the War in Europe.

UNITED STATES HOLOCAUST MEMORIAL MUSEUM United States National Museum for the commemoration of the Holocaust; situated on the Mall in Washington.

USTASHA National movement that came to power in Croatia in World War II.

VE DAY ("Victory in Europe") The day the Germans surrendered to the Allies—8 May 1945.

VERSAILLES TREATY Peace agreement ending World War I.

VICHY Town in France, headquarters of French government that ruled the unoccupied part of France.

VOLKSDEUTSCHE Germans living outside the borders of Germany.

WAFFEN SS Militarized units of SS.

WANNSEE CONFERENCE Meeting in a Berlin suburb on 20 January 1942 at which Nazi leaders drew up plans for the destruction of European Jewry.

WAR REFUGEE BOARD Body established by United States Presi-

dent Franklin D. Roosevelt to save people from Nazi Europe.

WARTHELAND (also War-the-gau) Region of western Poland which became part of Germany after September 1939.

WEHRMACHT The German army.

WEIMAR REPUBLIC Democratic regime in Germany from 1919 to 1933.

WORLD WAR I Armed conflict between 1914 and 1918 in which Germany and its allies (including Austro-Hungary and Italy) were defeated by the Allied countries (England, France, the United States from 1917, Russia until 1917).

WORLD WAR II Armed conflict between 1939 and 1945 in which Germany and its allies (Italy and Japan) were defeated by the Allied armies.

YAD VASHEM National Holocaust memorial of Israel; situated in Jerusalem.

YIDDISH Language of German origin spoken by many Jews in eastern Europe.

ZIONISM Movement for the return of Jews to Israel (Palestine). An individual member is a Zionist.

A B W E H R

The German High Command's foreign and counter-intelligence department. It was not directly charged with the murder of Jews, but one branch, the *Geheime Feldpolizei* (Secret Field Police), did participate in the massacre of Jews in the SOVIET UNION. Until 1944, it was headed by Admiral Wilhelm CANARIS, who secretly opposed Adolf HITLER. Canaris was executed in 1945 as a spy and a traitor.

AHNENERBE FORSCHUNGS UND LEHRGEMEINSCHAFT

("The Society for the Research and Teaching of Ancestral Heritage")

Organization founded by HEINRICH HIMMLER and others in 1935. The aim of the Ahnenerbe was to conduct historic and scientific research in "the sphere, spirit, deed and heritage of the Nordic Indo-Germanic race."

Before WORLD WAR II, much of this research was conducted on various pseudo-scientific and mystical topics.

With the outbreak of the war, however, these scientists began conducting many horrible experiments on prisoners. Human beings were injected with cancerous cells and exposed to high altitudes and freezing temperatures.

Several hundred Jewish and other prisoners died in these experiments. In one study, Hauptsturmführer (Captain) August Hirt, a professor of anatomy at Strasbourg University, collected human skulls from different races in order to make measurements and determine the differences between them. After he complained that he did not have enough Jewish specimens, 115 prisoners from AUSCHWITZ, including 79 Jewish men and 30 Jewish women, were promptly gassed and beheaded. Their skulls were added to Hirt's collection.

A J J D C

see AMERICAN JEWISH JOINT DISTRIBUTION COMMITTEE.

AKTION ("operation")

Term used by the Germans during the THIRD REICH, especially during WORLD WAR II, for any kind of special operation against actual or possible Nazi enemies. Like many other terms used by the Nazis, the word AKTION appeared to be a neutral term in the German language. It was therefore seen as a more fitting disguise for words like arrest, torture, robbery, and murder. During the Holocaust, an Aktion could mean the rounding up, deportation, and killing of Jews in their communities, as well as large scale mass murder in DEATH CAMPS or entire districts (for example, AKTION REINHARD). In the case of AKTION 1005, the term was used for the deliberate attempt to destroy any trace of the mass murders by digging up bodies and destroying them.

A K T I O N   1 0 0 5

Code name for the operation that attempted to remove all traces of the murderous activity of the Nazis throughout Europe. It began in June 1942 and continued through late 1944 in GERMANY, the annexed territories and all of the Baltic states (Estonia, Latvia, Lithuania).

Early in the summer of 1942, the vast number of hastily buried victims in the WARTHEGAU region in Poland constituted a health hazard to residents of the area. In addition, news of the mass murders had begun to spread to the Allied countries, leading to a Nazi desire to cover up their activities. Aktion 1005 was headed by SS-Standartenführer Paul BLOBEL, a professional architect, and carried out by the unit called SONDERKOMMANDOS 1005.

The initial phase of the operation involved burn-

> *...The extermination of the Jewish people...[is a] glorious chapter of our history...[that] should never be told.*
>
> *Heinrich Himmler*

ing the corpses in the CHELMNO death camp in June 1942. It was here that Blobel developed methods for burning corpses, crushing the bones and then scattering the ashes. The next phase began in June 1943. It involved opening mass graves and disposing of the bodies. The majority of this work was carried out by Jewish prisoners. The work consisted of three stages: first, the mass graves were opened and the bodies removed; second, the bodies were brought out and arranged on pyres and burnt; third, the ashes were sifted, the bones were crushed, the remaining valuables were removed and the ashes were scattered. In this manner as many as 2,000 corpses could be disposed of per pyre, daily.

Since Aktion 1005 had the status of "Reich secret," the prisoners performing the work were killed. The prisoners made numerous attempts to escape because many knew of their fate. For example, four members of the worker group at the Borki camp tunneled to freedom and, following the war, testified as to what they had seen at Borki. Although it resulted in the burning of millions of bodies, Aktion 1005 did not succeed in destroying all physical evidence of the mass murder. In the Klooga camp in Estonia, for example, not all the pyres had been set on fire by the time the Russian army entered the camp to liberate it. However, it did succeed in making it difficult to measure the full scope of the Nazi crimes. Blobel, the architect of Aktion 1005, stood trial at Nuremberg (see TRIALS OF WAR CRIMINALS) and was hanged on 8 June 1951.

AKTION ("operation") REINHARD

Code name for the German plan to kill more than 2 million people in central and southern POLAND (the GENERALGOUVERNEMENT). It involved the creation of three killing centers, also known as DEATH CAMPS— BELZEC, SOBIBÓR and TREBLINKA—in German-occupied Poland in 1942. It also referred to carrying out the killing program (1942–1943). The Aktion was named in honor of Reinhard HEYDRICH, head of the Reich Security Main Office (see REICHSSICHERHEITSHAUPTAMT). Heydrich had convened the WANNSEE CONFERENCE and was assassinated near PRAGUE in May 1942.

The timetable of Aktion Reinhard was swift. The camps were built in the first months of 1942. By the summer of that year, they were opened to begin murder operations against the Jews of Poland. The killing was by poisonous gas. All but a few of the people who arrived at one of these death camps were dead within hours. Within less than a year, the camps had fulfilled their function—the overwhelming majority of Polish Jewry was murdered, the GHETTOS were emptied and the death camps were prepared to be liquidated.

Belzec: Between March and December 1942, 600,000 Jews and several thousand Gypsies were murdered in the GAS CHAMBERS of Belzec. Only a few of those taken to Belzec survived.

Sobibór: More than 250,000 Jews were murdered in carbon monoxide gas chambers between May 1942 and July 1943. At the end of the war, there were only 50 survivors of Sobibór.

Treblinka: During the 14 months of Treblinka's operation, which began in July 1942, 870,000 Jews were murdered by a staff of 150, using diesel fuel. There were fewer than 100 known survivors of Treblinka. Of the staff, 30 were SS personnel, all veterans of the EUTHANASIA PROGRAM in GERMANY. They were assisted by 120 Ukrainians.

AKTION T4

SEE EUTHANASIA PROGRAM.

ALGERIA

Country in northern Africa. From the mid-nineteenth century, the country was governed by FRANCE. In 1870, the Jews of Algeria received French citizenship and were strongly influenced by French culture and education. In 1939, 117,000 Jews lived in Algeria.

In the summer of 1940, France was divided between the Nazi conquerors in the north and the pro-Nazi VICHY government in the south. Most of the French administration in Algeria declared loyalty to

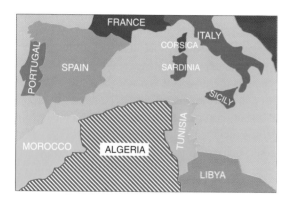

Antisemitic restrictions in Algeria were the most severe in all northern Africa, due to the personal beliefs of the high-ranking government officials. On 3 October 1940, a set of decrees severely limited the freedom of Jews in all walks of life. Four days later, Jews lost their French citizenship. In the same month, the Vichy government in Algeria put into effect the racial laws, which had already been passed in France according to the Nazi example. As a result, all Jews employed in governmental jobs were fired, and all Jewish students in state-owned schools were forced to leave. Jews were no longer allowed to own land and only a small number of Jews were permitted to work in professions such as medicine and law. On 8 July 1941, the government issued a decree ordering the registration of all Jews in Algeria. The Nazis built sixteen detention and FORCED LABOR CAMPS, and Jews were imprisoned there. In September 1942, the government established the General Union of the Jews of Algeria. It was similar to the European JUDENRAT. It was meant to help the Nazis control the Jewish community. It made it easier to recruit Jews for work. It was eventually used by the government to transport Jews to their death. In January 1942, Adolf EICHMANN ordered one of his most trusted men, Theodor Dannecker, to devise a plan for the DEPORTATION of Algeria's Jews to DEATH CAMPS in Europe. Dannecker's plan was to move them by sea from Algiers to Marseilles in southern France, and then by train to the final destination.

The Jewish community in Algeria survived, because of the early liberation of the country by Allied forces on 8 November 1942. The Allies' victory was speedy, because of the cooperation of the local underground group, which consisted largely of Jews (see box).

The liberation proved a disappointment. The Americans allowed the Vichy government to continue ruling and the anti-Jewish laws were not canceled. In December 1942, Jewish RESISTANCE leaders were arrested—on the orders of their former non-Jewish comrades in the underground movement. Only in March 1943, and under American pressure, were some racist laws canceled, while other anti-Jewish laws remained. General Charles DE GAULLE took over Algeria in May 1943. It was another three months before all the anti-Jewish laws were abolished.

In early 1941, a Jewish self-defense group established itself in Algiers disguised as a sports club. Other groups joined and contact was made with the United States army. A secret agreement was reached: when the Americans attacked Algeria the underground movement would liberate Algiers and the United States would assist it with arms. The date for the uprising was fixed for 7 or 8 November 1942. About 800 underground members—French and Jewish—were ready to participate, but the arms did not arrive from the Americans in time. Only 315 Jews and 62 Frenchmen took part in the end with the arms already in their possession. They had to cope with 11,000 armed French soldiers and policemen.

The underground split into six groups. The first was to take over police headquarters; the second, the army camp and navy headquarters; the third, army headquarters and the broadcasting station; the fourth, the house of the governor; the fifth the telephone operations; and the sixth was to capture Admiral Darlan, deputy premier of the Vichy government, who was visiting the country.

The underground accomplished most of its missions. It caused absolute havoc within the city of Algiers, and allowed the American army to land and take over the city with almost no casualties. The underground controlled the city for 20 hours and lost only one man, a Jewish officer.

Vichy. The head office of the Vichy administration for all of northern Africa was located in Algiers.

A L I Y A   B E T

Hebrew term for the organized immigration of Jews to PALESTINE in defiance of the British government's limitation on Jewish immigration.

The Balfour Declaration of 1917 and the LEAGUE OF NATIONS Mandate for Palestine of 1920 had both committed Great Britain to help in building a Jewish national home in Palestine. However, because of Arab pressure, the British government tried to pull back from this commitment in order to maintain peace in the region. As a result, increasingly severe restrictions were placed on *aliya* (Jewish immigration) during the years after the Arab riots of August 1929. In response, Zionists began a policy of *ha'apala* (literally, striving), or immigration without the benefit of immigrant certificates. While the British termed such immigration "illegal," the Zionists referred to it as *Aliya Bet*, second-type *aliya*, as opposed to (legal) *aliya*.

Aliya Bet first began in the mid-1930s in response to the steadily worsening situation for Jews in Europe. Initial attempts at such immigrations were made in 1934, but did not receive the support of the JEWISH AGENCY leadership. The official Zionist leaders opposed *Aliya Bet* at that time. Legal immigration had been allowed to increase somewhat in those years, so the leadership felt that the small number of immigrants arriving "illegally" could put the legal immigration at risk. They reasoned that if the British became angered by the "illegal" immigration, they would put a stop to the immigration they were already allowing. However, by 1937, when the British restricted legal *aliya*, both the Revisionist Zionists, followers of Vladimir Jabotinsky, and the *Hagana*, the underground militia of the Jewish Agency, established agencies to foster *Aliya Bet*.

In 1939, Jewish Agency Chairman David BEN-GURION called for an "*aliya* revolt" which he defined as a war for *aliya* to be waged by means of *Aliya Bet*. During WORLD WAR II, *Aliya Bet* became a primary means for rescuing Jews from the Nazis. Operations were severely hampered by lack of suitable ships and difficulties in finding trained crews. The continuing British blockade of Palestine and the generally unsafe conditions in the war zones and in

British soldier in Haifa facing the "illegal", immigrant ship "Theodor Herzl", 1947

the waters around them made the operations more difficult. After the war, *Aliya Bet* became the principal weapon in the Zionist rebellion against the British rule in Palestine. Whenever they could, the British stopped the boats from bringing these immigrants to Palestine and sent them to detention camps in Cyprus. In one case—the ship EXODUS 1947—they sent the Jews back to DISPLACED PERSONS camps in GERMANY. With public opinion as its main tool, the leaders of the Palestine Jewish community used *Aliya Bet* to display to the world the bankruptcy of British policy regarding Palestine. This led to the United Nations' ultimate decision on 29 November 1947 to create a Jewish state. Altogether 115,976 Jews arrived in Palestine under the framework of *Aliya Bet*.

A L I Y A T   H A N O A R

see YOUTH ALIYA.

A L S A C E - L O R R A I N E

see FRANCE.

AMERICAN FRIENDS SERVICE COMMITTEE (AFSC)

QUAKER agency established in 1917. In the years following World War I, the AFSC provided food to over one million CHILDREN in GERMANY. It expanded its European operations by setting up centers in BERLIN, VIENNA, and PARIS.

During the 1930s, especially after 1938, the AFSC provided valuable aid to those seeking to leave Germany. At first, it hesitated to criticize the Nazi government's policies. However, it provided other organizations, such as the AMERICAN JEWISH JOINT DISTRIBUTION COMMITTEE with reports about what was going on in Germany. Working with the Jewish agencies, the AFSC offered assistance to victims of Nazi persecution. After KRISTALLNACHT of November 1938, it worked with European Quakers, Jewish agencies, and other groups to bring about 10,000 Jewish and Christian children from Germany and AUSTRIA to GREAT BRITAIN.

In the UNITED STATES, the AFSC also set up training and orientation programs for newly arrived REFUGEES.

When WORLD WAR II broke out in Europe, the AFSC continued its activities to aid Nazi victims. In unoccupied FRANCE, the Quaker agency and other groups provided food and vitamins to over 84,000 children being held in French internment CAMPS. In 1941 and 1942, the AFSC helped to evacuate over 300 children from France. In the neutral countries of SPAIN and PORTUGAL it aided refugees who were trying to flee from Europe. In 1944, it called for temporary refugee camps to be set up in the United States. When President Franklin D. ROOSEVELT established FORT ONTARIO, New York, as an "emergency refugee shelter," the AFSC provided assistance to people housed there.

After the war, the AFSC provided some assistance to DISPLACED PERSONS (DPs) in Europe. On a larger scale, it shipped food, clothing, medicine, and other essentials to civilians in the western zones of occupation in Germany. In the United States, the AFSC, with other organizations, lobbied Congress to pass emergency DP laws to allow the admission of hundreds of thousands of European refugees. For its work during and after the war, the American Friends Service Committee and its counterpart, the British Friends Relief Service, received the Nobel Peace Prize in 1947.

AMERICAN JEWISH JOINT DISTRIBUTION COMMITTEE (JDC; "Joint")

American charitable organization created in 1914 to send money to Jews overseas who were in need. During the Holocaust, the JDC (or AJJDC) became the central Jewish relief body involved in relief and rescue activities.

Between 1933 and 1937, most JDC funds were spent on aid to Jewish communities in GERMANY and eastern Europe, for relief and emigration. After 1938, there were more and more refugees. The JDC took over the costs of helping Jews move to areas that seemed safer. It worked by supporting HICEM (an American agency for assisting emigrants), and through its own channels. Before the Americans entered the war in December 1941, the JDC used a cash transfer arrangement to make it possible for Jews to leave Europe. Those leaving would give their money to local Jewish relief organizations and

JDC worker fitting Polish refugee with a new pair of shoes. Berlin, Germany 1946

in exchange the JDC would pay for their passage in dollars. Programs were also set up by the JDC in countries that received Jews. This included aid to some 125,000 refugees who had reached South and Central America and the Caribbean. After the fall of FRANCE in June 1940, the JDC moved its European headquarters from PARIS to Lisbon. Some 90,000 Jewish refugees were able to escape via Lisbon during the war.

Most of the JDC's budget between 1939 and 1945 was spent on relief and rescue activities within occupied Europe. Support to Polish Jews was sent through the JDC's WARSAW office. Money was used to relieve conditions in GHETTOS and to help thousands of Polish Jews who had fled the advance of the German army. JDC money sent to France was used by local organizations for relief and rescue activities. The establishment of the WAR REFUGEE BOARD (22 January 1944), paid for mainly by the JDC, centralized rescue work. It allowed the JDC to continue sending money from New York to Lisbon and SWITZERLAND. During 1944, the JDC spent large amounts on aid to Hungarian, Slovakian and Romanian Jewry.

Looking at the JDC's success in fund-raising in America is one way of measuring how involved American Jews were in the Holocaust. It is surprising that despite intense fund-raising campaigns, the JDC annual budget *decreased* yearly between 1938 and 1942. Thus, only $6 million were available for distribution in 1942, compared with over $12 million in 1939. After the war, the JDC's budget increased. This allowed it to carry out many relief programs in Europe and to support refugees in DISPLACED PERSONS camps.

AMERICAN JEWRY AND THE HOLOCAUST

At the time of the Nazi rise to power (early 1930s), most JEWS living in the United States had been born in Europe. Many of the others were the first generation to be born in the United States. They were trying to make their way into American society, by adopting the English language and American culture. They were seeking to establish their careers despite widespread ANTISEMITISM. Many did not want to stress their Jewishness for fear of endangering their welcome into a new culture. Charles Coughlin, a Roman Catholic priest, Henry Ford, the automobile millionaire, and Charles Lindbergh, the aviation hero, were among the most famous public figures to declare antisemitic views. They were not alone. Frequently, American Jews were afraid to speak out against antisemitism.

For American Jewry, it was a new experience to have their Jewish brothers in other countries look upon them as world Jewish leaders. This trend had begun during World War I, but even then they shared the partnership with Europe. Until the early 1930s, European Jewry had been the focus of the Jewish world for 1,000 years. With the outbreak of WORLD WAR II this changed and Jews everywhere looked to United States Jewry for leadership.

American Jewry was not prepared for the role. It lacked any central representative organization like those found in other countries. American Jews were divided in their backgrounds, their groups, and their approaches to the rise of Nazism. The leadership of the American Jewish Committee—the older, established families of German origin—called for quiet diplomacy. They were unhappy about the idea of boycotts and public demonstrations, which were favored by the American Jewish Congress. Jews were divided among Zionists, non-Zionists and anti-Zionists. The first called for a Jewish state in PALESTINE (Israel) and the second were interested in Palestine as a haven for REFUGEES. The anti-Zionists strongly opposed a Jewish home in Palestine. Ultra-Orthodox Jews went their own way and founded the VA'AD HA-HATSALA ("Rescue Committee"), which did everything it could to rescue students and rabbis of academies of advanced Jewish learning (*yeshivot*) from Europe. A militant group called the BERGSON GROUP (after Peter Bergson, which was the name adopted by its leader, Hillel Kook, a Jew from Palestine), publicly pressed for the rescue of Jews. It placed large advertisements in newspapers and organized mass demonstrations.

All these differences meant that American Jewry spoke in many voices. (An attempt was made to coordinate efforts on behalf of Jews of Palestine and other countries at the American Jewish Conference, founded in 1943. It only lasted a few years.) The only real field of unification was fund-raising. The United Jewish Appeal, established just before the war, became the central Jewish charitable organization. It collected $124 million between 1939 and 1945.

At the time, American Jewry did not have the powerful pressure groups that developed after the period of the Holocaust. Rabbi Stephen S. WISE, president of the American Jewish Congress, did not have access to President Franklin D. ROOSEVELT. He had to use other Jews who were close to the president as intermediaries. As a result, American Jewry did not have the power to pressure the government to admit refugees before the war began in 1939. This remained true during the two terrible years of persecution in Europe before the United States entered the war in December 1941. Only in the eleventh year of Nazi rule did Henry J. MORGENTHAU Jr., secretary of the treasury, who was a Jew, persuade the president to establish the WAR REFUGEE BOARD. Morgenthau did this after he was given a shocking memo by three non-Jewish members of his staff, called "On the Acquiescence of this Government to the Murder of the Jews."

Jewish support for President Roosevelt and his policies—both domestic and foreign—was high. He knew he could rely on 90 percent of the Jewish votes.

Roosevelt appealed to Jewish patriotism by stressing that nothing should be done to hurt the war effort. His policy was that the refugee problem should be tackled only after the war was won. He was helped in his lack of action by disagreements among Jews, who argued instead of taking action.

Was the Nazi threat really one of GENOCIDE? Should there be a Jewish army? Should AUSCHWITZ be bombed (see AUSCHWITZ BOMBING)? What should be the agenda for postwar Jewry? At the same time, some have expressed doubts that American Jews could have changed the course of events very much, even had they been more united and aggressive. (See also UNITED STATES AND THE HOLOCAUST.)

AMERICAN PRESS AND THE HOLOCAUST

The first serious reports that were written about the NAZI PARTY in American newspapers described Adolf HITLER's rise to power and his racial theories of Aryan superiority (see RACISM). Some journalists were particularly anti-Hitler in their reporting, but many of these were later influenced by German diplomats, as well as by their editors at home, to change their positions. However, others insisted on reporting the true situation. H. R. Knickerbocker, from the *New York Evening Post*, was expelled from GERMANY for his stories. Also expelled was Dorothy Thompson, who wrote a regular column for the *Philadelphia Public Ledger*. In August 1934, she wrote: "My first offense was to think that [Adolf] Hitler is just an ordinary man. That is a crime against the reigning cult, which says that Mr. Hitler is the Messiah sent by God to save the German people. To question this mystic mission is so terrible that if you are a German you can be sent to jail. I, fortunately, am an American. I merely was sent to Paris." Germany was sensitive to foreign press reports and was interested in the world's response to German policies.

In November 1938, press reports about KRISTALLNACHT appeared on the front pages of nearly every major newspaper in the Western world. The *New York Times* ran headlines on it for nearly a week. As a result of this press coverage the United States withdrew its ambassador to Germany.

After war broke out, in September 1939, it became more difficult for journalists to cover news stories in areas under German occupation. It was not clearly known what was happening to the Jews until November 1942. At that point, Rabbi Stephen S. WISE, then president of the WORLD JEWISH CONGRESS, held a press conference and gave proof that the Jews of Europe were being murdered in DEATH CAMPS (see box for headlines).

For the next two years, limited coverage of Nazi murders appeared in world newspapers. After the

---

Headlines from newspapers dated 25 November 1942

2 MILLION JEWS SLAIN BY NAZIS, DR. WISE STATES

Chicago Tribune

WISE SAYS HITLER HAS ORDERED 4,000,000 JEWS SLAIN IN 1942

New York Herald Tribune

JEWISH EXTERMINATION DRIVE LAID TO HITLER BY DR. WISE

Baltimore Sun

Headlines from newspapers dated 26 November 1944

U.S. CHARGES NAZIS TORTURED MIL-LIONS TO DEATH IN EUROPE—War Refugee Board Says 1,765,000 Jews Were Killed by Gas in One Camp Alone: Witnesses' Testimony Gives Details of the Atrocities

New York Herald Tribune

INSIDE STORY OF MASS MURDERING BY NAZIS—Escapees Give Detailed Accounts of the Gassing and Cremating of 1,765,000 Jews at Birkenau—From an Official Publica-tion of the War Refugee Board

Louisville Courier Journal

U.S. BOARD BARES ATROCITY DETAILS TOLD BY WITNESSES AT POLISH CAMPS

The New York Times

---

establishment of the WAR REFUGEE BOARD in January 1944, more reports describing the murder of the Jews made it to the press (see box).

With the end of the war and the liberation of the CAMPS, people were shocked to see the first pub-lished photographs of the Nazi murder machine.

Some historians criticize the press coverage as too limited in scope. They have shown that the cover-age that did appear was far too little, considering both the huge scale of the tragedy and the amount of available information. They say that ANTISEMITISM on the part of the United States State Department influenced the views of editors of major American newspapers, magazines, and radio. They also write that there may have been some anti-Jewish feeling among the journalists and editors themselves, which caused them to limit stories about the Nazi murders.

ANIELEWICZ, MORDECHAI

(1919 or 1920–1943) Commander of the WARSAW GHETTO UPRISING. Anielewicz was born in WARSAW. As a youth he joined the Ha-Shomer Ha-Tsair Socialist

Statue of Mordechai Anielewicz in kibbutz Yad Mordechai, Israel

Zionist movement and became one of its leaders. After the Germans occupied POLAND in 1939, he went to VILNA in Lithuania, where many Zionist youth had gathered. Some of them, including Anielewicz, volunteered to return to German-occupied Poland to lead the movement's activities.

In the summer of 1941, upon receiving reports of the murder of Jews in the German-occupied areas of the SOVIET UNION, Anielewicz pushed for the creation of an armed Jewish underground. In the summer of 1942, he went to Bedzin in western Poland to help establish an armed underground. Shortly after, the mass DEPORTATIONS in Warsaw began. He returned to Warsaw to discover that only about 60,000 Jews remained and that the new armed underground organization, the JEWISH FIGHTING ORGANIZATION (ZOB), was weak. He set about restructuring the organization, and in November 1942, became its commander.

The first armed battles between the Jews and the Germans occurred during the deportation drive of 18 January 1943. In a brief battle, in which many Jewish fighters fell, Anielewicz was saved by his men. The deportation ended rather quickly, and the Jews of Warsaw believed it was Anielewicz's fighters who had caused the Germans to abandon their operation. On the eve of Passover (19 April 1943), the Germans began their final deportation drive in Warsaw. The armed underground reacted with all the weapons that it had. Anielewicz commanded the fighting. With most of his staff, he entered a bunker. On May 8, amid the burning ruins of the ghetto, he was killed when the bunker fell to the Germans. Mordechai Anielewicz is considered one of the outstanding heroes of the Holocaust. Kibbutz Yad Mordechai in Israel is named for him.

ANNE FRANK HOUSE

The house where Anne FRANK and her family hid in Amsterdam. It has become a place of pilgrimage for visitors from all over the world. A constant stream of people climb its narrow staircase, pass the revolving bookcase which concealed the hiding place and then go up to the rooms where the family lived. Of special interest is Anne's own room, the walls of which are still decorated by the postcards and cutouts that she stuck on them. The house also

Anne Frank House in Amsterdam

Bookcase in the Anne Frank house which closed to hide the stairs leading up to the attic where the Frank family hid

Statue of Anne Frank beside the bookcase

has an exhibition on the Frank family. The original first album of the diary and other manuscripts by

Anne Frank are on display. Another exhibition is devoted to the evil of antisemitism.

The Anne Frank House is operated by a foundation devoted to fighting all forms of racism. It organizes programs based on its exhibitions. An exhibition showing the life of Anne Frank has been seen in many countries. The foundation produces teaching material relating to today's multiethnic societies and the fight against prejudice and racism.

Its address is Prinsengracht 263, Amsterdam, the Netherlands.

A N S C H L U S S

The German word for "union" or "annexation" that was used for the unification of AUSTRIA and GERMANY on 13 March 1938. By marching into Austria, Germany officially rejected the 1919 Paris Peace Conference which had recognized the Republic of Austria.

The West viewed the *Anschluss* as an invasion. Germany and Austria saw it as the cultural and social reunification of Greater Germany. Huge crowds turned out to welcome Adolf HITLER back to his native land.

German troops entering Vienna on 13 March 1938

ANTI–JEWISH LEGISLATION

Over 2,000 laws were passed by the Nazis against the Jewish population between 1933 and 1943. Already in 1920, the new Nazi Party had announced its goals, including its antisemitic program. The Nazis thought that Jews should not be German citizens and should not hold public office. Also, any Jews who had moved to GERMANY after 1914 should be made to leave. No new Jewish immigration should be allowed. In 1933, the Nazi Party came to power and began to put its program into action. The Nazis made it legal to discriminate against Jews.

Anti-Jewish legislation went through three phases. The first was between 1933 and 1935. On 7 April 1933, the Law for the Restoration of the Civil Service was passed. This divided Germans into "Aryans" and "non-Aryans" (see RACISM). Non-Aryans were people with at least one non-Aryan (for example, Jewish or GYPSY) parent or grandparent. The law meant that non-Aryan, especially Jewish, civil servants could be dismissed from their jobs. Further laws were passed to bar Jews from other professions, including law and journalism. In July 1933, a law took away the citizenship of Jews who had moved to Germany after 1914. Educational opportunities were taken away from many Jews. They were banned from taking final exams so that they left school without qualifications. JEWISH RELIGIOUS LIFE was also attacked when ritual slaughter of kosher meat was made illegal in April 1933. In this period, Jews were banned from many organizations, social clubs, and public baths.

In September 1935, the second phase of the legislation began with the passing of the NUREMBERG LAWS. These laws separated Aryans, Jews, and MISCHLINGE (those with both Jewish and German ancestors) and gave each of them a different status. Jews were deprived of German citizenship by the Reich Citizenship Law. They lost the right to vote. The law for the Protection of German Blood and German Honor made marriage and sexual relations between Aryans and Jews or Gypsies illegal. Law after law was passed, which further restricted the freedoms of the Jewish community. In 1937, most Jewish students were removed from German schools and universities and restrictions were placed on Jews traveling abroad. In 1938, all Jews had to add either "Israel" or "Sarah" to their names to identify them as Jews.

The third phase of the legislation began in November 1938. Its special goal was to take the Jews' wealth from them and seize it for the Nazis. After the KRISTALLNACHT pogrom, the Jewish community as a whole was fined a billion reichsmarks by the Nazi state to pay for repairs (of the damages caused by the Nazis). On 12 November, a decree was issued to eliminate the Jews from German economic life. Jews were barred from most occupations in German society. Other laws were passed that allowed the majority of Jewish-owned businesses to be seized by the Nazis and Aryanized (see ARYANIZATION). Jewish institutions were abolished and Jewish affairs were taken over by the Reich Association of Jews in Germany, controlled by Reinhard HEYDRICH and the SS.

Bench in a German park marked "for Jews Only"

The Nazis encouraged Jews to leave the country. However, since the state had stripped most Jews of their savings, emigration was difficult for many. Those who stayed were further excluded from society. After the outbreak of war, life became even more unbearable. Jews were banned from having radios or telephones and from using public transportation. From September 1941, all Jews had to wear an identification BADGE in public. In October 1941, a law banned Jewish emigration, and in the same month the first DEPORTATIONS of German Jews to DEATH CAMPS began.

When Germany invaded AUSTRIA on 13 March 1938 (see ANSCHLUSS), all the anti-Jewish laws that had been passed in Germany since 1933 were immediately forced on Austrian Jews. Anti-Jewish legislation was also applied to all other countries occupied by Germany. They were most harsh in POLAND.

ANTISEMITISM

Term coined in 1879 by the German Wilhelm Marr to describe hatred of Jews. The phenomenon of Jew-hatred goes back to the ancient world. In Christian lands, antisemitism took on religious overtones, based on the belief that the Jews had been responsible for the death of Jesus and were therefore all god-killers. This took on many forms—ideological, in the development of anti-Jewish stereotypes (e.g., the Jew was equated with the devil), and practical expressions ranging from expulsions to massacres. The 19th century saw the emergence of a new form of antisemitism, based not on religious ideas, but on racial theories (see RACISM). In particular, there emerged the (scientifically unsound) theory of "superior" and "inferior" races. The ARYANS were seen as the super race, while the "Semites" were the most inferior race ("Semites" was applied almost exclusively to Jews—other Semitic peoples, such as the Arabs, seldom featured in these theories). An outgrowth of the new ideology was a pseudo-science that sought to prove anthropologically the superiority of the Aryans over the Semites (see EUGENICS). Marr and other antisemites argued that if Jews were allowed total freedom, they would eventually dominate GERMANY and the world.

This belief was then supported by a new myth—the conspiracy theory. This found wide circulation in the creation of a forgery, the PROTOCOLS OF THE ELDERS OF ZION, which held that Jewish leaders were plotting to control the world. These ideas spread quickly and, in 1881, a petition by an Antisemitic League demanding that Jews lose their civil rights received a quarter of a million signatures.

Antisemitism in the 20th century was encountered throughout the world. In addition to the religious and "racial" roots, there were economic reasons including jealousy of the progress of Jews after they had received civil rights. The Russian Bolshevik Revolution of 1917, in which a number of Jews were prominent, led many in the West to identify Jews with Bolshevism. Indeed, Adolf HITLER in his attacks

Jews made to carry a sign saying "we are the scum of the earth," in Poland

Sign saying "Jews not wanted in these places," Germany, 1935

on Jews, without bothering to explain the contradiction, condemned Jews as "capitalists and Bolsheviks." He used a combination of traditional Jew-hatred and modern antisemitism. He preached the danger of Jewish infiltration into German society and also the classic stereotypes of the Jew as the defilers of Christian maidens and murderers of Jesus.

Antisemites in many countries in the 1930s founded fascist or Nazi-type organizations sympathizing with Hitler and his aims. They used his techniques and vocabulary to attract support and were to be found under different names, such as Cagoulards in France, Rexists in Belgium, British Union of Fascists in Britain and several similar bodies in the United States. They were particularly successful in east European countries and founded the Arrow Cross party in Hungary.

Once he came to power, Hitler implemented increasingly intensive antisemitic policies, ranging from racial laws (see NUREMBERG LAWS) to extermination, and these were applied by the Germans and their supporters in every country that they controlled.

After WORLD WAR II, with the realization of the extent and horror of the Holocaust, there was a feeling of revulsion in many quarters. Some Christian groups, for example, introduced new teachings aimed at uprooting traditional religious antisemitism. Governments no longer enacted antisemitic laws or policies. Groups that followed fascist and Nazi policies tended to be small and marginal. At the same time remembering that the Nazi party had started as a small group, Jews everywhere were watchful of the potential threats and dangers of antisemitism. There were, however, two blocs of countries where official antisemitism continued to be a threat. One of these was Soviet Russia and its satellites. Joseph STALIN became paranoid about Jews and after the war introduced an anti-Jewish persecution that only ended with his death in 1953. Under this influence, antisemitic manifestations occurred in various communist countries—and could even be found in places where Jews no longer lived. Another source was in Muslim—especially Arab—countries. Hostile feelings toward Jews had been made worse in the 20th century by opposition to Zionism and the State of Israel. Arab countries continued to disseminate the *Protocols of the Elders of Zion*, which is still read—even in Japan—by many, despite its exposure as a forgery over 70 years ago. As antisemitism became unfashionable after the war, the communist and Muslim worlds advocated a policy of anti-Zionism, which was often, however, a disguise for antisemitism. Another form taken on by contemporary antisemites is Holocaust denial (see HOLOCAUST, DENIAL OF THE).

> *One day a Jew passed the Roman Emperor Hadrian who was furious: "You a Jew dare to greet the Emperor! You shall pay for this with your life!" Later that day, another Jew passed the Emperor and did not greet him. "A Jew dares pass a Roman Emperor without saluting?" Hadrian exclaimed, "You shall be killed!" To his puzzled courtiers, Hadrian explained, "I hate Jews, so I use any excuse to destroy them."*
>
> *The Talmud*

ANTONESCU, ION

(1882–1946) Military and political leader of ROMANIA. Antonescu served with distinction in the Romanian army during World War I. In 1937, he was minister of defense in the government led by Octavian GOGA. In 1940, Romania had to give up territories to SOVIET

Ion Antonescu (standing in center) as a war criminal in his trial in Moscow after the War

RUSSIA, HUNGARY, and BULGARIA. After this crisis, Romania's King Carol named Antonescu "Conducator"—i.e., leader or guide of the country, like other fascist rulers of the time (see FASCISM AND FASCIST MOVEMENTS). In September 1940, Antonescu met with Adolf HITLER. Antonescu called on German troops to enter the country, supposedly to defend Romania against the Soviet threat.

Antonescu's policy toward the Jews was complex. He kept up a dialogue with representatives of Romanian Jews and refused to let JEWS from prewar Romania be deported. He did, however, ruin their economic life and persecute them severely. He was also responsible for the mass murder of the Jews in the rural areas of BESSARABIA and BUKOVINA and the deportation of the survivors to TRANSNISTRIA. Under his orders 10,000 Jews were killed in the Ukrainian port of Odessa—at that time under Romanian rule. On 23 August 1944, Antonescu was arrested upon the order of Romania's King Michael (Carol's successor), who handed him over to the Soviets. He was sentenced to death at a TRIAL OF WAR CRIMINALS in May 1946 in Moscow and executed.

Antonescu is still considered a hero by a large number of Romanians. Since the fall of the Ceaucescu regime in 1989, attempts are being made to clear Antonescu's name. Without waiting for an official decision in the matter, a number of streets in the country have been given his name.

APPEASEMENT

The policy of appeasing Adolf HITLER and Benito MUSSOLINI during 1937–1939 by continuously tolerating their territorial annexations. This was done in the hope that it would help end the expansionist policies of these dictators. The acceptance of the Italian conquest of Ethiopia in 1937, the toleration of the German annexation of AUSTRIA in 1938, the lack of help to the Spanish Republic during the Spanish civil war of 1936–1939, and the MUNICH AGREEMENT of 1938, all formed part of this policy. Its aim was to avoid war.

Appeasement was pursued in particular by the British government under Prime Minister Neville Chamberlain and to some extent by the French government. Its most important opponent was Winston CHURCHILL, who foresaw that the policy would only increase the appetites of the dictators for more territory. Another opponent was British Foreign Secretary Anthony Eden, who resigned his post in protest in February 1938. Appeasement came to an end

At the Munich Conference, September 1938. From left to right (in front) Neville Chamberlain, British Prime Minister; Eduard Daladier, French Prime Minister; Adolf Hitler, German Führer, Benito Mussolini, Duce (leader of Italy) and Italy's Foreign Minister Galeazzo Ciano

Entrance gate to Auschwitz death camp, above which appear the words "Arbeit Macht Frei"

when Hitler, ignoring the promise he had given at Munich, seized CZECHOSLOVAKIA in March 1939. With this, Chamberlain decided on a new policy of resistance to German aggression.

"ARBEIT MACHT FREI" ("Work Makes One Free")

Motto posted over the gates of AUSCHWITZ and other CONCENTRATION CAMPS. It is an example of the doublespeak used by the Nazis to mask their true intentions. Prisoners were expected to understand from the sign that work in the camp would both rehabilitate them and benefit the THIRD REICH. Its message was that by working hard, prisoners would be spared the degradations they had experienced in occupied Europe. Indeed, many prisoners believed that the concentration camps were part of a vast "resettlement" and "labor" program for Jews, and for other "undesirable" elements in Germany. Clutching onto every last hope, they would then make the trek to selection and, for many, the showers (gas chambers) and ovens.

A R G E N T I N A

Country in South America. Argentina passed its first restrictive laws on immigration just before Adolf HITLER became chancellor of GERMANY in January 1933. The world's economic crisis and growing nationalism, intolerance, and ANTISEMITISM were sweeping the country. This influenced Argentina's official attitude toward the immigration of Jewish REFUGEES during the time of the Holocaust. In 1933, German JEWS were trying to leave Germany. Argentina maintained that its laws did not recognize the category of "refugees," i.e., those forced to move. They would only consider "free" immigrants, and gave preference to farmers. In 1938, when the demand for havens for European Jews grew more desperate, Argentina's regulations became more rigid. The government issued a secret memo calling for stricter laws to be applied to applicants who were already under consideration, particularly if they were Jewish. Later in the same year, following KRISTALLNACHT and throughout 1939, Jewish refugees obtained immigration visas to various other Latin American countries. In many cases, these were slightly irregular to protect the identities of the consuls who sold them. When the immigrants arrived in Buenos Aires lacking regular Argentinian transit visas, they were often sent back to Europe. This occurred even in 1941 and 1942.

Argentina maintained its neutrality even after the Japanese attack on Pearl Harbor in December 1941. At that time, other Latin American nations either declared war on or broke relations with the Axis Powers (GERMANY and ITALY). Not until January 1944, did the Argentinian government, pressed by the United States, break its relations with Germany. It did not declare war until the war was coming to an end, in March 1945.

Argentina had many opportunities to intervene on behalf of Jews, because of its continued contacts with the Nazis and its importance for German interests in the Western Hemisphere. However, Argentina did very little. On 20 November 1942, the Argentinian government officially announced its willingness to help. Yet Argentina did not even try to use its influence with the Nazis to rescue the CHILDREN it declared itself willing to save.

It is estimated that the immigration of Jews to Argentina throughout the Nazi period amounted to between 35,000 and 39,000 persons. This includes illegals who crossed the borders from Paraguay, Bolivia, and Uruguay, and those who remained in the country beyond the time of their temporary visas. The immigrants who arrived during the time of the Holocaust made important contributions to the development of the largest Jewish community in Latin America.

After the war, Argentina became a major haven for Nazi war criminals. Eventually, a few were sent to Europe for trial. The most notorious, Adolf EICHMANN, was kidnapped by Israelis in Buenos Aires and taken to Jerusalem for trial. Many thousands of Nazis managed to hide their identity and live the rest of their lives without being touched.

ARMÉE JUIVE ("Jewish Army"; AJ)

Jewish RESISTANCE group in FRANCE, later called Organisation Juive de Combat (OJC), or "Jewish Fighting Organization." It was created at the beginning of 1942 by a number of Zionist groups. They were inspired by the words of group member David Knout, who published a pamphlet in July 1940 called "*Que faire?*"—("What to do?"). In it he restated the motto of the United States as: "We are seventeen million Jews in the world. United we constitute a strength. Divided, we are food for massacre." Members swore allegiance to the Zionist flag and pledged to fight for the rebirth of ISRAEL. They saw themselves as a fighting organization more than an organization of self-defense. At first, the AJ failed to get support among most French JEWS, who did not realize the danger that they were in. After the mass arrests in PARIS on 16 July 1942, it attracted many more members, although it never had more than 2,000 at any time. Even so, it had some success because its members were all well-integrated French Jews who had a wide network of contacts at all levels of French society. They were thus able to operate an escape route to SPAIN. This route was first intended for young Jews going to PALESTINE, and ended up saving hundreds of people. The AJ provided countless others with fake documents, which allowed them to avoid arrest. At the same time, the AJ sabotaged railroads, bridges, factories, and other targets, including GESTAPO officers. In March 1944, it launched one of its most famous operations, a surprise attack that killed Gestapo informers in Nice. The AJ trained fighters who fought with French resistance forces.

In the summer of 1944, the Gestapo arrested most of the Paris members of the network. Although they were tortured, they gave no information. They were sent to the DRANCY CONCENTRATION CAMP on their way to the DEATH CAMPS in POLAND. Fourteen of them managed to jump from the train and escape. In August 1944, the AJ participated in the general uprising against the Germans in the main cities in France.

ARROW CROSS

Hungarian fascist movement. In 1935, Ferenc SZÁLASI founded the Party of the National Will which became the Arrow Cross Party in 1939.

It was a violently antisemitic organization, responsible for many attacks on Jews. It was suppressed from 1939 to 1941, but when the Germans occupied HUNGARY in March 1944, the Arrow Cross received support from the new governement and became popular in the country. In October 1944, Admiral Miklós HORTHY sought to take Hungary out of the War and the occupying Germans immediately put the Arrow Cross in power, declaring Szálasi head of state.

During the three months it was in power, the Arrow Cross murdered some 20,000 Jews in BUDAPEST and sent about 70,000 on the "DEATH MARCH" to GERMANY.

Leaders of the National Council of Hungarian Fascist Arrow Cross Party celebrate after their leader, Ferenc Szálasi, became head of state, October 1944

ART IN THE HOLOCAUST

The secret art produced in the CAMPS and GHETTOS during the Holocaust was created under impossible conditions with makeshift materials and often at the risk of the artists' lives. There are several reasons why artists produced art under such circumstances.

First, art was a form of spiritual RESISTANCE to the Nazis' efforts to dehumanize their victims. Through art, artists maintained a link with their former identity—a link the Nazis tried to break by constantly humiliating the prisoners. Artists expressed their individuality through the act of creation. They asserted control over their materials and over their choice and treatment of the subject. For example, some illustrations of the camps give no hint of what life was really like there. By making small changes, the artists brought order and normalcy into their lives, at least in their pictures. Thus, Louis Ascher drew children seated beside the barracks in BERGEN-BELSEN as though they were relaxing in a summer camp. This approach is expressed in Charlotte Buresova's wish "to oppose the disaster with beauty." It also explains the art of CHILDREN in the ghettos: they were told to paint pleasant scenes to raise their morale.

Art was also seen as a way to affirm life itself. Jozef Szajna said that the trace of himself that he left on paper would survive even if he perished. This goal explains the large number of self-portraits which reproduce both the artists' features and their emotions. Samuel Bak's haunting *Self-Portrait at the Age of Thirteen* (1946) depicts the boy-artist wide-eyed in horror, still seeing the hell he had survived

Samuel Bak, Self-Portrait at the Age of Thirteen

Bedrich Fritta's son Tommy perched on a trunk looking out the window at a symbol of freedom

The Selection. The trucks waiting for their victims. Alfred Kantor

before him. The need to affirm life also explains the many portraits of inmates. Their main purpose was to state that the person had existed even if he or she died among a mass of nameless victims. Many who posed wished to be remembered in a somewhat idealized way. However, there are also realistic portrayals of the old and the sick, captured on paper shortly before their deaths.

Expressions of hope and the desire for freedom come from the need to affirm life. They also help one to gather the courage to continue to live despite everything. These ideas are expressed in Bedrich Fritta's drawings for his son Tommy's third birthday. The series opens with Tommy, standing on a trunk, which symbolizes his wanderings. He is looking out the window at a symbol of freedom: a bird flying over the roofs of THERESIENSTADT. Other drawings show the careers he may choose. This was wishful thinking in 1944, since the odds were that he would not survive. Fritta drew Tommy playing among flowers, butterflies, and birds under a smiling sun. On the drawing he wrote: "This is not a fairy tale. It's true!"

Another major goal of camp and ghetto art was to act as an eyewitness report. This challenged the German's wish for secrecy. Thus, 12-year-old Helga

Weissova-Hoskova's father told her: "Draw what you see." Many artists said that they were not creating art but, in Karol Konieczny's words, "a shocking document of a world of horror and torment. I want the young to know how it was, so that they...will not allow such conditions to ever be repeated." Young Alfred Kantor added another idea: "My commitment to drawing came out of a deep instinct of self-preservation.... By taking on the role of an "observer" I could at least for a few moments detach myself from what was going on in AUSCHWITZ and was therefore better able to hold together the threads of sanity." Such artists showed everything, from the miserable living conditions in the ghettos; to the cattle cars, selections, and brutal camp labor; to the DEATH MARCHES, GAS CHAMBERS, and corpses. These works provide more information on the Holocaust than film-clips and photographs. They document scenes for which there is no other record.

Being an eyewitness, however, is not simple. The artist must choose not only *what* to depict, but *how* to depict it. The artist could choose to be an objective realist, portraying how camp life *actually* looked. On the other hand, artists could choose to be expressionists, altering the image to convey their subjective *feelings*. Most artists decided on straight description, but a few made other choices. The way that different artists drew the many-tiered bunk beds in the camps can serve as an example. Boris Taslitzky chose to draw BUCHENWALD inmates lying in the beds realistically. By contrast, Auguste Favier tried to reveal the harshness of the bunk-beds' deeper meaning. He used the beds as a background for expressionistic living "skeletons." His drawing suggests the slow draining away of life that took place at Buchenwald. Fritta expressed the same message by setting the beds into a niche, like shelves in a burial cave. The beds' standing supports became bars which imprison the dying inmates. Thus, for Fritta the bunk beds symbolized death traps.

Catharsis (the expression of anger and pain over a harsh experience in an attempt to unburden oneself) was especially important to help the artist to recover after the Holocaust. Many artists drew camp scenes over and over again until they felt free from their terrible experiences.

The situation in Theresienstadt was special. Fritta and the other artists there were forced to produce art for their German overseers in a naturalistic style. For them, this forced naturalism became a style of lies, through which they helped the Nazis create the fraud of the "model camp." They reacted by producing their own secret work in an expressionistic style. Their secret art exposed the starvation and death that lay behind the supposedly normal life in the camp. This function of their art is clear in Fritta's *Film and Reality*. The background to the picture is a film made by the Nazis which pretended to show that life in Theresienstadt was ideal. The film showed the concerts, coffeehouse, and a bank created for the RED CROSS visit to the camp in 1944. In fact, after the film was completed, the Jews who had been forced to make it were shipped to Auschwitz. In Fritta's picture, a Jewish beautician, who grows out of her table, applies make-up on a sad Jew, while being filmed by a camera wearing stormtrooper boots. Behind the curtain, Fritta draws a skeleton lying in a CONCENTRATION CAMP, which tells the truth behind the film's facade.

Witnessing through art is thus a complex experience. The artists wished to create not only documents of how the camps looked, but—equally important—about how they themselves felt about being trapped by the Holocaust.

ART OF THE HOLOCAUST

Art as a reaction to the Nazi persecution of the JEWS, began to appear in 1933, after Adolf HITLER's rise to power. This art continued through the Holocaust to the present day. It was created both by artists who had experienced aspects of the Holocaust and by those who had not. It includes artists of different religions and nationalities who worked in various styles. Despite this diversity, they used similar themes both in depicting and in interpreting events.

Some of these themes were provided by the photographers who accompanied the camp liberators. Their widely published images turned everyone who saw them into an eyewitness. They recorded the mounds of the dead, the deathly thin bald survivors barely able to stand, and the inmates crowded behind barbed-wire fences. These images became identified with the Holocaust in the public imagination and strongly influenced non-inmate artists. However, portrayals of people behind barbed wire were already common in art from the mid-1930s, since artists in all countries knew that the CAMPS were surrounded by barbed-wire fences. This image remains strong to this day. It reappeared in George Segal's *Holocaust* (which is in New York's Jewish Museum and outside San Francisco's Palace of the Legion of Honor) as a clear symbol of the camps.

Other common themes in non-inmate art had a shorter life span. REFUGEES were popular subjects in the 1930s and 1940s, since artists knew this subject first hand, either through observation or because they themselves were refugees. The subject disappeared from art after 1948, because ISRAEL was seen as a solution to the refugee problem. The theme of Jewish RESISTANCE and especially the WARSAW GHETTO UPRISING was popular during and immediately after the war in many countries. After the Israeli War of Independence (1948), this subject also almost completely disappeared.

The image that created the deepest, most lasting impression on artists, whether or not they had experienced the Holocaust were the mounds of corpses which also posed the greatest artistic and emotional problems. Haunted by this gruesome image, artists sought ways to translate it into art.

Mordecai Ardon, Sarah. Crying out at God in anguish on finding her son dead on the altar

Statue by Nathan Rapaport commemorating the Warsaw Ghetto Uprising in Yad Vashem, Jerusalem

They usually followed the lead of Pablo Picasso, whose *Charnel House* dealt with the theme by using semi-abstraction. Another approach was to concentrate on isolated groups of corpses, reducing the mass to establish a more personal contact for the spectator. This would help the viewer overcame the horror long enough to take in the artist's message. Christians freely used the photographs as a basis for their art works. However, Jewish artists, such as Hyman Bloom, preferred other visual sources for the in images of death.

Certain objects from the camps became symbolic of the whole camp experience. For example, placing a crematorium chimney (see GAS CHAMBERS, GAS VANS, AND CREMATORIA) in a painting, immediately gave it a camp context, even when no camp was shown. Samuel Bak set one on an island dominated by the dice of chance to suggest his understanding of his Holocaust experience. Strands of barbed wire also immediately call up the Holocaust. Igael Tumarkin used such strands in abstract reliefs to add a Holo-

caust meaning. This symbol is so well known that it is used in other contexts to suggest the Holocaust: Marc Klionsky wrapped barbed wire around a Russian Jew to symbolize his imprisonment in Russia, which he thus suggested was like a CONCENTRATION CAMP.

From the early 1930s, artists also created noncamp images to point out the different moral lessons to be learned from the Holocaust. Jacques Lipchitz symbolized Jewish resistance to the Nazis by sculpting David killing a Nazi Goliath. He used the Greek myth of Prometheus slaying the vulture to inspire non-Jews to resist Nazism, because it threatened everyone, not only the Jews. In some statues Lipchitz emphasized a physical resemblance between Prometheus and the vulture, suggesting that Nazism is an evil within every human that must be defeated.

Various biblical images were used to convey different views of the Holocaust victim. Mordecai Ardon used the Sacrifice of Isaac in this way. He portrayed

Sarah crying out at God in anguish on finding her son dead on the altar, while Abraham mourns helplessly in the background. Job, who demanded that God explain the tremendous suffering that had befallen him, also became a symbol of the Holocaust victim. Ivan Mestrovic's deathly thin Job accuses God, while Nathan Rapaport's Job, with a concentration camp number on his arm, retains his faith despite everything. The most frequent symbol of the Holocaust victim, from the 1930s on, was the crucified Jewish Jesus. With this image, the artist—be he a Christian like Otto Pankok or a Jew like Marc Chagall—warned Christians that they crucified Jesus again when they slayed his Jewish brothers. After the war this image was also used to denounce the CHRISTIAN CHURCHES for not doing enough to save the Jews.

Artists who tried to represent the Nazi aggressor found that portraying him realistically only expressed the "banality of evil" (the idea that Nazi evil was "ordinary"). Following the lead of John Heartfield and George Grosz, they therefore revealed the Nazis' true nature by symbolizing them as monsters or as Death. However, after the Holocaust, artists began to understand, as had Lipchitz, that evil was not limited to the Nazis. Matta and Francis Bacon combined victim and oppressor in one image. This implied the gloomy idea that all of mankind tends toward evil. Maryan, an embittered survivor of AUSCHWITZ, turned all of humanity into monsters exuding excrement.

Maryan's reaction raises the problem of the art of the survivors. Some continued to document the Holocaust, believing that it was their duty to the dead to record their agony. Many artists, however, felt they had freed themselves from their experiences by depicting them obsessively just after the Holocaust. They turned their backs on their past to become engrossed in art. A few, such as Avigdor Arikha, maintain this position. After working for years in abstract expressionism, he now focuses exclusively on everyday reality. Most artist-survivors, however, eventually returned to dealing with the Holocaust, often inspired by events such as the EICHMANN TRIAL or the frequent massacres in various parts of a world that have learned nothing from the past. Thus, in the 1970s, Zoran Music based a series of works on his 1945 drawings of corpses in DACHAU, feeling that—as the title says—*We Are Not The Last.*

As opposed to the survivors, assimilated Jewish artists who did not experience the Holocaust first hand reacted to it by returning to their roots. From the 1940s on, artists such as Ben Shahn and Jack Levine began using biblical themes, praying men, Jewish village scenes, and Hebrew inscriptions. On the other hand, younger artists, such as R. B. Kitaj, lacking a Jewish education, affirm their Jewish identity by dealing with the Holocaust.

This difference in generations can also be seen in the reactions of artists' to the connection between Israel and the Holocaust. In the late 1940s, Chagall and Lipchitz saw the creation of the State of Israel as a solution to the plight of the survivors. However, the constant wars fought by Israel and the threats to its existence in 1967 and 1973 led some artists to see in every conflict a renewal of the Holocaust.

Holocaust images have also been used by some artists to make statements about current conflicts. By this they aim to show that the current oppressors are like Nazis and the victims are like Holocaust victims. As we approach the year 2000, the fear that man is about to destroy himself has led artists such as Music and Robert Morris to use Holocaust images in another way. They show Holocaust corpses in order to warn the world that disaster looms and that it can be prevented if we act before it is too late.

Recently, children of survivors—such as Yocheved Weinfeld and Haim Maor—have tried to describe in art what their own reactions would have been had they experienced the Holocaust. At the same time, German artists have begun to deal with their country's past. Anselm Kiefer stresses that this must be done so that healing may begin. Both he and Maor also deal in their art with the complex relationship between Germans and Jews created by the Holocaust.

ARYAN/ARYANISM

SEE RACISM.

ARYANIZATION

The process of transferring Jewish businesses to German ownership throughout GERMANY and the annexed territories from 1933 to 1943. It refers to both the progressive removal of Jews from the economic life of the German Reich and the seizing of Jewish assets by the state.

Prior to Aryanization, Jews were actively involved in the economic life of Germany. Estimates of the number of Jewish businesses in Germany in 1933 exceed 100,000. These included retail stores, factories, newspapers, publishing houses and private professional practices.

Beginning in 1933, a widespread economic boycott (see BOYCOTT, ANTI-JEWISH) was imposed by the German government. It first targeted the retail stores and then moved against the professions. The boycott was steady, and at times violent. It had the result of forcing the majority of Jewish businesses to fail or to be sold for a fraction of their worth. By April 1938, only 39,552 Jewish retailers remained in business.

The first stage of Aryanization was an unofficial campaign of intimidation. Tactics such as posting signs condemning the support of Jewish busi-

Pianos confiscated under Aryanization laws from the Jewish population in Prague 1939

> The basic idea of Aryanization of the economy is this: The Jew is removed from the economy and transfers his economic property to the state. He gets compensation. The compensation is registered in the debit registry, and he gets a certain interest on it (3.5%). That is what he is to live on.
>
> Hermann Göring

nesses, harassing customers by patrols in uniform and posting names and pictures of Germans who patronized Jewish businesses were used. Local chambers of commerce monitored Jewish businesses so that Nazi Party members could get the best ones for themselves. In Austria, for example, more than 80 percent of Jewish businesses were taken by local political leaders. By contrast, in France, only one-third of the Jewish businesses were taken because of a reluctance on the part of local leaders to cooperate. However, after KRISTALL-NACHT and the pogroms of November 1938, legislation was passed making Aryanization a matter of law in countries under Nazi rule. Jews, and those married to Jews, were required to register all of their valuable property (real estate, jewelry, works of art, businesses) with the Nazis, and were forbidden to buy or sell without permission. This prepared the way for Jewish assets to be officially confiscated by the state.

The impoverishment of the Jews, which resulted from Aryanization, made them even more undesirable as citizens. The idea of having to support the Jews was, of course, hateful to the Nazis. Emigration was encouraged. Hermann GÖRING observed in October 1938, that Jewish GHETTOS would have to be set up in the large cities. The establishment of Jewish slave labor brigades was also suggested at this time.

Following the assassination of a German diplomat in Paris by Herschel GRYNSZPAN, an "atonement payment" of 1 billion RM (reichsmarks) ($400 million) was demanded of the Jewish community. This was taken in the form of a tax on individuals. At this time, all insurance money owed to Jews for damages sustained during the Kristallnacht pogroms were seized by the Reich. The Jews would have to bear the cost of repairs. An "escape tax" was imposed on those emigrating. Jews leaving the country were forced to place their money in an "emigration account," under GESTAPO control. Eventually, these funds were seized by the Reich. Jews deported to THERESIENSTADT were forced to sign a "home purchase agreement" with the Reich Association of Jews in Germany, which guaranteed to take care of them for the rest of their lives. This deal cost either 1,000 RM ($400) or all of their remaining assets. In November 1941, all property of deportees was confiscated to pay for the cost of the "FINAL SOLUTION". By 1943, with escape routes now closed, the remaining assets of those deported to labor and death CAMPS were used to finance their own destruction.

A U S C H W I T Z

The largest and the most deadly of the Nazi DEATH CAMPS. It was located in the Polish town of Oswiecim, 37 miles west of Kraków. Auschwitz was actually three camps, in one: a FORCED LABOR camp, a CONCENTRATION CAMP and a death camp.

Chief of the SS Heinrich HIMMLER ordered the establishment of Auschwitz in April 1940. It opened in June for Polish prisoners. Until 1 March 1941, the population of Auschwitz was about 10,900 people, mostly Poles.

The character of the camp changed in March 1941, when Himmler ordered a death camp to be built less than two miles away. It was named Birkenau after the nearby birch trees. It is estimated that more than 1,250,000 people were murdered there, mostly in the gas chambers. One million one hundred thousand Jews, tens of thousands of Poles, 19,000 GYPSIES, and 12,000 SOVIET PRISONERS OF WAR were killed at Birkenau.

The third part of Auschwitz was the slave labor camps built nearby. Large German companies, such as I.G. FARBEN and Daimler Benz, built huge plants there in order to profit from the cheap and seemingly endless supply of slave labor. The largest slave labor camp was Buna-Monowitz, also known as Auschwitz III, where synthetic rubber was produced.

The first GAS CHAMBER was erected in Auschwitz I. It began operating on 3 September 1941. Six hundred

Soviet prisoners of war and 250 other prisoners were gassed. When Birkenau opened, four gas chambers were built. Bodies were burned in specially built crematoria designed for the massive needs.

Jews were deported (see DEPORTATIONS) to Birkenau from all over Europe, often in freight cars. When they arrived, an SS doctor would divide the young and the able-bodied from other prisoners. This process was known as "selection." Those chosen to die were sent directly to the gas chambers. Their personal possessions were taken. As many as 2,000 were forced into the sealed gas chambers at one time. SS men would pour two canisters of ZYKLON B gas down an opening, and within 20–30 minutes the new arrivals would be dead. Their bodies would then be sent to the crematoria, where gold teeth were removed before they were cremated. Sometimes, when the crematoria could not handle the volume of killings, bodies were burned in open fields.

The able-bodied who had passed the first selection were then processed. Their hair was shaven, their personal belongings confiscated and a number tattooed on their forearms. From then on they would be referred to by number, not by name. They were forced to work long hours, under terrible conditions. Prisoners suffered from very poor food, clothing and shelter. They too faced "selections" from time to time. Only the few able to withstand these horrible conditions could survive. Weakened or sick prisoners were sent back to Birkenau and gassed.

In March 1944, GERMANY occupied HUNGARY. Between 14 May and 8 July, 437,402 Jews were deported to Auschwitz on 148 trains. Most were killed within days of their arrival. The capacity of Auschwitz was stretched to the extreme.

STERILIZATION experiments were carried out in Auschwitz by an air force physician, Dr. Horst Schumann. Dr. Josef MENGELE became the camp's chief physician in November 1943. He tried to "prove" the superiority of the ARYAN race. He experimented on Gypsy children and then on twins, dwarfs and persons with abnormalities (see MEDICAL EXPERIMENTS).

Inmates of Auschwitz attempted to resist the Nazis. There were several escapes from Auschwitz. The most important was by two Slovakian Jews,

Above: Auschwitz barracks. Below: Footwear and other personal effects taken from the prisoners in Auschwitz before they were sent to the gas chamber

Selected groups of prisoners were sent to the gas chambers to be put to death. For several months we saw long processions of people going to their death; the biggest groups were exterminated in May, June, and July, 1944. In that period the crematoriums were busy day and night, as could be seen from the flames issuing from the smokestacks. We could often smell burning flesh, hair or nails. At that time, besides the fire from the chimneys of the crematoriums, we saw two large bonfires. From the camp came the barking of SS watchdogs. Since the crematoriums were overloaded, the unfortunate victims were led up in groups, and at the sight of the bonfires guessed what was in store for them. I knew that my relatives had suffered the same fate and that I myself would not escape it. Approximately every two weeks the camp doctor Mengele selected new victims. One day 500 children were murdered. Heart-rending scenes took place when these children were sent off, since everyone knew by then where they were going.

Professor Berthold Epstein from Prague University quoted in 1945:
The Year of Liberation, published by the U.S. Holocaust Memorial Museum

Rudolph Vrba and Alfred Wetzler. They left on 7 April 1944 with detailed information about the structure of the death camp and the upcoming deportation of Hungarian Jews. They brought this news to the Jewish underground in Slovakia, which passed it on to the Allies.

On 7 October 1944, the SONDERKOMMANDO (prisoners forced to empty the gas chambers and work the ovens), blew up one of Birkenau's four crematoria. A complicated underground network had been set up to smuggle dynamite to the *sonderkommando*. The explosion was followed by the mass escape of 600 prisoners.

Four young women were accused of supplying the dynamite. They were hanged in the presence of the other prisoners. One of them, Roza Robota, shouted in Hebrew—"*hazak v'ematz*" ("be strong, have courage")—as the trap door was opened.

In mid-January 1945, the Nazis knew that the Russian army was approaching. They marched most of the 67,000 remaining prisoners a long distance and then sent them by freight trains to the GROSS-ROSEN, BUCHENWALD, DACHAU, and MAUTHAUSEN concentration camps. Those too ill to march were left behind at Auschwitz to die. Almost one in four people died during these DEATH MARCHES. The Germans worked frantically to take Auschwitz apart. Crematoria buildings were blown up, SS documents and I.G. Farben Company records were destroyed, and 29 storerooms were burned. On 27 January 1945, the Soviet army entered Auschwitz. In the six storerooms that remained, the Soviets discovered

348,820 men's suits, 836,255 women's coats, more than seven tons of human hair, and even 13,964 carpets, which had been brought by victims who did not realize their fate.

There were several postwar trials of Auschwitz staff. A Polish court tried Rudolf HÖSS, the commandant of Auschwitz during its most important periods. He was sentenced to be hanged on 2 April 1947 on a gallows set up outside the crematoria at Auschwitz I. In November and December 1947, a Polish court tried 43 Nazis. Twenty-three were sentenced to die and 16 were sent to prison. Between 1963 and 1966, German courts tried additional Auschwitz staff.

Today, the camp contains a museum, housed in some of the original barracks, and memorials to its victims. Visitors from many countries come in large numbers to the site. It has become a place of pilgrimage, especially for young people (see YOUTH PILGRIMAGES TO HOLOCAUST SITES). The word Auschwitz has come to symbolize in many languages the cruelty and horror of the Holocaust itself.

AUSCHWITZ BOMBING

During the spring and summer of 1944, hundreds of thousands of Hungarian Jews were deported to AUSCHWITZ-BIRKENAU. As many as 10,000 people were killed each day in its GAS CHAMBERS.

In mid-April, two men escaped from Auschwitz and brought detailed information, including maps of Auschwitz, to Jewish leaders in Slovakia. These leaders then demanded that the Allies bomb Auschwitz and the railroads leading to it in order to stop or slow down the killing process.

The request triggered fierce debate. Some were afraid of killing innocent civilians. Some did not want to give the Germans a reason to blame the Allies for the deaths of Jews. Others could not fully grasp the reality of daily gassings at Auschwitz, even when they had accurate information.

The requests that were made by Jewish leaders to bomb Auschwitz were denied. Various reasons were given: Auschwitz was not within the range of Allied bombers; resources should not be diverted from the war effort; bombing Auschwitz might lead to even more vengeful German actions.

There is still debate today among historians and military analysts whether Auschwitz could have been bombed. During the summer of 1944, Buna, a FORCED LABOR factory less than five miles east of the gas chambers, was heavily bombed. This disproves the claim that Auschwitz was not within range.

The United States War Department decided, in January 1944, that units of the Armed Forces would not be "employed for the purpose of rescuing victims of enemy oppression," unless such rescues took place in the course of routine military operations.

A War Department memo of February 1944 advised: "We must constantly bear in mind that the most effective relief which can be given the victims of enemy persecution is to ensure the speedy defeat of the Axis." Yet this defeat came too late for those murdered in 1944–1945 at Auschwitz.

AUSCHWITZ TRIAL

see TRIALS.

AUSTRALIA

Continent in the Southern Hemisphere, between the Pacific and Indian oceans. Before the Nazis came to power in GERMANY, the Australian Jewish community was small and isolated from the rest of the Jewish world. In 1933, the community numbered 23,000 and its only connection with other communities was through British Jews.

Australia had an immigration policy called "White Australia," which was designed mostly to keep out immigrants of non-British origin. Even so, from the mid-1930s onward, a number of Jewish refugees found their way to Australia. The terrible treatment of Jews in Germany led some Jewish leaders to request that the Australian government accept Jewish immigrants from Europe. The government refused. The Australian representative to the 1938 EVIAN CONFERENCE would not accept any refugees. Later, however, the horrors of KRISTALLNACHT made a great impact and led to a change in policy. The Australian government agreed to accept 15,000 refugees. Between 1933 and 1945, some 8,200 refugees, most of whom were Jewish, made their way to Australia. Included in this number are the refugees (classed as "enemy aliens") deported from Britain on the boat DUNERA. Australia's membership in the British Commonwealth led the country to enter the war on the side of the Allies in September 1939.

After the war, Australia's immigration policy began to encourage immigrants of non-British origins, although the preference for "white" immigrants remained. Between 1947 and 1959, over 700,000 individuals arrived in Australia, including approximately 17,300 Jews. This postwar immigration changed the nature of the country in general. The Jewish immigrants also had a positive impact on the nature of Jewish life in Australia. They brought elements of the richness of European Jewish life to Australia.

The wave of postwar immigrants also included a number of war criminals. They lived in Australia in safety for decades, until a War Crimes Bill was enacted in 1988, partly because of pressure from the Jewish community. This law created the possibility of prosecuting people who committed war crimes outside of Australia. The government's Special Investigations Unit examined the histories of hundreds of individuals who had become Australian citizens. Some efforts were made to prosecute them, but were unsuccessful.

Today, the Australian Jewish community has the largest proportion of Holocaust survivors of any Diaspora community. Jewish and non-Jewish artists have addressed Holocaust themes, and Australian writer Thomas Keneally wrote *Schindler's Ark*, the book upon which the Steven Spielberg film on Oskar SCHINDLER, *Schindler's List*, was based.

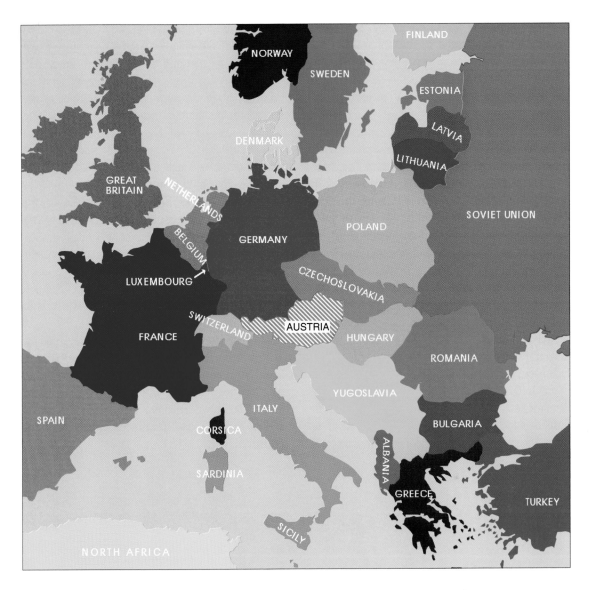

A U S T R I A

Country in central Europe which became independent in 1918 with the break-up of the Austro-Hungarian Empire. Its population in 1937 was 6.75 million, including just under 190,000 Jews. It shares its western border with GERMANY.

Jews in Austria were almost fully integrated into the country's culture. From the middle of the 19th century, Jews had equality of civil rights and the right to organize as a community. Austria was a center of Jewish culture, counting among its prominent citizens Theodor Herzl, the father of modern Zionism. Jews such as the psychiatrist Sigmund Freud played a major role in making Vienna one of the great cultural cities of the world. At the same time, antisemitism existed side by side with emancipation. Both Adolf HITLER and Adolf EICHMANN were born in Austria and were influenced by this antisemitism.

On 12 March 1938, Hitler invaded Austria and made it a part of Germany. This was known as the ANSCHLUSS. The Nazis were welcomed enthusiastically by most of the Austrians. The same pattern of anti-Jewish riots, economic persecution, social isolation and brutality seen in Germany during the previous five years now began in Austria. The Austrian Nazis proved as cruel as their German counterparts. Within the week after the *Anschluss*, Jewish community offices in Vienna were closed, community officers and prominent people were jailed, and widescale looting of Jewish homes and businesses began. This was followed by the removal of Jews and spouses of Jews from public employment and service in the army. Synagogues were desecrated and a heavy sum was imposed on the Jewish community.

The process of ARYANIZATION, the systematic taking of Jewish-owned property by the government, proceeded at an accelerated pace in Austria. The Property Transfer Office, whose sole purpose was to seize Jewish assets, opened in Vienna in 1938. There had been more than 26,000 Jewish businesses in Austria, but within four months nearly all of those in the countryside and one-third in Vienna had been seized. This was accompanied by mass dismissals of Jews from their jobs. The economic ruin of the Jewish community, imposed officially and executed with enthusiastic local cooperation, served another goal: to force the emigration of the Jews from Austria. In August of 1938, under Adolf Eichmann, the Central Office for Jewish Emigration opened. This office took the remaining property from the Jews and processed their departure.

Austrian Jews suffered like German Jews during the KRISTALLNACHT. In Vienna alone, 42 synagogues were burnt down and over 4,000 Jewish stores were looted. Eichmann ordered Jews imprisoned in CONCENTRATION CAMPS in order to force enormous additional payments and to speed up emigration. When a person was released from prison, he or she had a certain amount of time to leave Austria. If he did not leave, he or she would be imprisoned again. However, visas to other countries were scarce, and the struggle to obtain one added to the people's panic and demoralization. Large numbers of Jews were trapped in Austria, paving the way for the DEPORTATIONS and mass-murder that were to follow.

The effectiveness of the measures taken against the Jews of Austria prior to the outbreak of the war can be calculated: two thirds of the Jewish population emigrated (126,500) with an additional 2,000 escaping during the war. Over 65,000 Austrian Jews were murdered.

Following the war, only 1,747 Jews returned to Austria from the concentration camps. Of those, many were survivors from other parts of Europe who had been brought to Austria as slave laborers. Some 1,000 Jews remained alive in Vienna but, by and large, the Austrian Jewish community had been destroyed.

B A B I   Y A R

Huge valley on the outskirts of KIEV in the UKRAINE, near the site of Kiev's local Jewish cemetery. At this spot tens of thousands of Jews were rounded up and murdered by the Nazis on 30 September 1941. Babi Yar is an example of the work of the mobile killing forces, the EINSATZGRUPPEN which the Nazis put into action after their invasion of the SOVIET UNION.

Memorial monument at Babi Yar

On 28 September 1941, notices were distributed by the Germans around the city of Kiev ordering all Jews to meet the following morning for resettlement. The Jews gathered and were marched down to the Jewish cemetery bordering the ravine of Babi Yar, which had been surrounded by barbed wire by the Germans. When the Jews arrived, all men, women and children were ordered to register and to turn over all of their valuables. They were then forced to strip and to move to the edge of the ravine in groups of 10. As each group reached the

edge, it was mowed down by machine guns. Every so often the bodies were sprinkled with dirt. The gunners were rotated every few hours. During the course of 48 hours, 33,771 Jews were murdered.

From then until the end of the war the ravine was used as a murder site for over 100,000 people, the vast majority of whom were Jews. Also killed at Babi Yar were people who tried to save Jews, GYPSIES and SOVIET PRISONERS OF WAR.

In July 1943, the Nazis tried to destroy all evidence of the murders at Babi Yar. As part of AKTION 1005, Jewish prisoners were forced to dig up bodies, burn them and then sift through the ashes for jewelry and other valuables. On 29 September 1943, the prisoners became aware that they too would be killed at Babi Yar when their work was done. The next morning, at the first fog, 25 of them ran for their lives, and 15 made it to safety. They lived out

No gravestone stands on Babi Yar;
Only coarse earth heaped roughly on the gash....

On Babi Yar weeds rustle;
The tall trees
Like judges loom and threaten...
All screams in silence.
I take off my cap.
And feel that I am slowly turning gray.
And I too have become a soundless cry.
Over the thousands that lie buried here.
I am each old man slaughtered,
Each child shot,
None of me will forget.

Excerpts of poem entitled Babi Yar written by
the Russian poet Yevgeny Yevtushenko
Translated by Marie Syrkin

the remainder of the war in hiding in the forest.

After the war, no memorial was built at Babi Yar. This was the subject of a protest poem by the Russian poet, Yevgeny Yevtushenko. It was not until 1974 that a memorial was built. It, however, failed to mention that Jews had been victims. Only in recent years has a new memorial been built which refers to the Jews.

BACH-ZELEWSKI, ERICH VON DEM

(1899–1972) ss general in charge of warfare against PARTISANS.

Bach-Zelewski joined the Nazi Party in 1930. He was an early member of the SS and one of its highest-ranking officers at the outbreak of WORLD WAR II. After the German invasion of Russia in 1941, he commanded one of the EINSATZGRUPPEN charged with mass murdering Jews in BYELORUSSIA. In 1943, he was appointed commanding officer of German forces fighting against partisans in eastern Europe.

Bach-Zelewski was a key witness in the TRIALS OF WAR CRIMINALS at Nuremberg. He testified that brutality against civilians was the product of direct and repeated orders from the highest levels of the Nazi military. He also said that detailed reports of these activities were sent back by field commanders to the central command. His testimony contradicted the claims of members of the high command that the field commanders had operated independently.

Bach-Zelewski was tried after the war in GERMANY, drawing a 10-year prison sentence. Released after five years, he was again tried in 1961 and this time received life imprisonment for murder dating back to 1933 when Nazis were fighting communists in the streets.

Why, that dirty, bloody, treacherous swine.... He was the bloodiest murderer in the whole goddamned setup! The dirty, filthy schweinhund ("pig-dog"), selling his soul to save his stinking neck!

Outburst of defendant Hermann Göring at Nuremberg, following Bach-Zelewski's testimony

---

B A D G E

A symbol often in the form of a yellow Star of David, which Jews were forced to wear during the Holocaust. Like many other restrictions imposed by the Nazis upon Jews, the badge was not an original concept. In most Christian and Muslim countries during the Middle Ages, Jews were forced to wear certain articles of clothing to distinguish and isolate them from other people. This often took the form of a badge.

The Nazis first introduced the badge in GERMANY on 1 April 1933, when a national boycott of Jewish shops was instituted (see BOYCOTT, ANTI-JEWISH). Jewish shopkeepers were ordered to identify their

These badges and markings in the collection of the United States Holocaust Memorial Museum were used by the Nazis to isolate targeted groups. Yellow stars and triangles were for Jews, purple triangles for Jehovah's Witnesses, red triangles for political prisoners, black triangles for Gypsies and pink triangles for homosexuals. Letters generally indicated the nationality of a prisoner and the name of a camp

Wedding in Amsterdam, The Netherlands, 1941. The participants are wearing the Jewish badge

establishments by painting large yellow stars on their front windows. The German Zionist leader, Robert Weltsch, wrote a famous essay in a German Jewish newspaper entitled: "Wear The Yellow Badge With Pride." In his essay (see box on this page), he argued that the Star of David, now intended as a symbol of degradation, should instead become a symbol of Jewish pride.

After the war began in September 1939, Jews living in Nazi-controlled areas throughout Europe were forced to wear yellow stars on their outer clothing. In POLAND, LITHUANIA, HUNGARY, BULGARIA, and parts of GREECE, a simple yellow star was attached. In Germany, the star was black on yellow. In Alsace, BOHEMIA, and MORAVIA, the yellow star bore the word *"Jude,"* in FRANCE it read *"Juif,"* and in HOLLAND, *"Jood"* (all meaning "Jew"). In the rest of Greece, Belgrade, and Sofia, the Nazis instituted a yellow

April 1, 1933 (the beginning of the anti-Jewish boycott), will remain an important date in the history of German Jewry—indeed in the history of the entire Jewish people. The events of that day have aspects that are not only political and economic, but also moral and spiritual.

A powerful symbol is to be found in the fact that the Nazi leadership gave orders that a sign "with a yellow badge on a black background" was to be pasted on the boycotted shops. This regulation is intended as a brand, a sign of contempt. We will take it up and make it a badge of honor.

Many Jews suffered a crushing experience on Saturday. Suddenly they were revealed as Jews, not as a matter of inner avowal, not in loyalty to their own community, not in pride in a great past and great achievements, but by the impress of a red placard with a yellow patch. The patrols moved from house to house, stuck their placards on shops and signboards, daubed the windows.

In addition to other signs and inscriptions one often saw windows bearing a large Magen David, the Shield of David the King. It was intended as dishonor. Jews, take it up, the Shield of David, and wear it with pride!

Excerpts from an article published by Robert Weltsch
in a Zionist Weekly, Jüdische Rundschau, 4 April 1933

armband. In parts of POLAND, a blue star on a white background was worn as an armband and in SLOVAKIA, it was a blue star on a yellow background. There are also examples of metal tags with the letter "J" being used to identify Jews. Other condemned groups also had to wear special identification (see illustration).

BAECK, LEO

(1873–1956) Reform Rabbi and leader of German JEWS during the years of Nazi persecution. He served as a Liberal (Reform) rabbi in Berlin, where he also taught at the Reform rabbinical seminary. His writings on Jewish theology were admired by many. He was seen as one of the outstanding Jewish thinkers of his time.

After serving as a military chaplain in the German army in World War I, Baeck became a leading member of numerous German Jewish organizations in WEIMAR Germany. Under the Nazis, an overall German Jewish organization, the REICHSVERTRETUNG DER DEUTSCHEN JUDEN, was formed in 1933. Baeck became its president and held this office until its successor organization (the Reichsvereinigung) was dissolved in 1943. Although many advised him to leave GERMANY,

Leo Baeck

he refused to go as long as there were Jews left there. In 1943, he was deported to the THERESIENSTADT CONCENTRATION CAMP, where he continued to serve as a spiritual leader. His dignity and positive attitude greatly strengthened the morale of his fellow prisoners. After his liberation in 1945, he lived in London. He often taught in the United States, at the Hebrew Union College in Cincinnati, Ohio.

BANDERA, STEFAN

(1909–1959) Leader of the Ukrainian National Movement (OUN). Bandera became a nationalist leader in the UKRAINE in the early 1930s. He was jailed for his activities in 1936. When he was released in 1939, he continued his nationalist efforts. Bandera and his comrades hoped that by cooperating with the Germans they could establish an independent Ukrainian government. He formed two Ukrainian battalions to help the Germans before they invaded Russia. However, when the OUN announced that it was forming a Ukrainian government on 30 June 1941, the Germans were not supportive. Bandera and several others were arrested and sent to the SACHSENHAUSEN CONCENTRATION CAMP, where he remained until late 1944. After the war, he lived in Munich, where he was murdered by a Soviet agent in 1959.

BARASCH, EPHRAIM

(1892–1943) Head of the JUDENRAT (Jewish Council) in BIALYSTOK in northeast POLAND.

The Bialystok GHETTO was established at the end of July 1941, when 35,000 Jews were placed there. Barasch, first the assistant head, and later the head of the Judenrat, developed a policy to save the ghetto. He established industries that the Nazis required for supplying their occupying forces. He insisted that his workers be efficient, and convinced ghetto residents not to sabotage the industry. He explained that the more essential they were to the Nazi war effort, the more likelihood they had of surviving. At the same time, Barasch maintained close relations with the underground movement and with the Zionist Youth Movement within the ghetto. For example, he gave funds to the Zionist Youth underground and to their leader Mordechai TENENBAUM to

From the political point of view, the main danger of the Bialystok Ghetto is that it is the largest and most populous one [in the district]. Steps have to be taken so that our 35,000 inhabitants achieve justifications [for their existence], so that we may be tolerated. We have transformed all our inhabitants into useful elements. Our security is in direct proportion to our labor productivity. We already have 20 factories in operation. Any day now, there will be opened a weaving factory, a factory making wooden lasts, a woodwork and a wheel factory....

From a speech by Ephraim Barasch at a mass meeting of the Bialystok ghetto, June 1942.

buy materials for making their own weapons.

In order to insure that the ghetto remained productive, Barasch also had to supervise the DEPORTATIONS of Jews to DEATH CAMPS. He straddled the two extremes—support of the underground on the one hand, and the deportation of "non-productive" Jews on the other. He hoped that, when the time came to liquidate the ghetto, he would have enough notice to inform the underground and to join their uprising.

On 16 August 1943, large-scale deportations from the Bialystok ghetto began. This sparked off the ghetto uprising, which lasted five days, but was finally suppressed by the German troops. Between 21 and 27 August, 25,000 Jews were deported to their deaths at TREBLINKA. Barasch and several hundred Jews were not sent to Treblinka, and remained in Bialystok. In November 1943, they were deported to MAJDANEK. Details of Barasch's fate are unknown.

BARBAROSSA, OPERATION

Code name for the sudden invasion by Nazi Germany of SOVIET RUSSIA, begun on 22 June 1941. It was named after the medieval German emperor, Frederick I, known as Barbarossa ("Red Beard"), a legendary figure in German folklore.

Adolf HITLER had made a 10-year non-aggression pact with the Russian ruler, Joseph STALIN, in 1939. However, Hitler later felt threatened by the Soviet occupation of the Baltic states and eastern Romania. In addition, Nazi ideology had long spoken of

German troops waiting to cross a river in their invasion of Russia (Operation Barbarossa), 1941

> We have to divide up this vast cake [Russia] properly, so as to enable us:
> 1. to rule it
> 2. to administer it
> 3. to loot it.
>
> Adolf Hitler on Operation Barbarossa

destroying Bolshevism and obtaining LEBENSRAUM (living space) at the expense of Russia.

Operation Barbarossa introduced a new stage in the Holocaust. There were over 3.5 million Jews in Soviet Russia, including inhabitants of the Baltic states and Polish refugees. The murder of these Jews was seen as an important part of the operation. To deal with this new "Jewish problem," specially-trained troops, the EINSATZGRUPPEN, were charged with the massacre of the Jews in the newly acquired territories. They carried out this task with cruel efficiency (see WORLD WAR II).

BARBIE, KLAUS

(1913–1990) German Nazi. Head of the GESTAPO in Lyon after the Nazis took over southern FRANCE on 11 November 1942.

Barbie joined the Nazi party in 1932 and the SS in 1935. In 1941–1942, he operated against the JEWS of Holland. Under his guidance, 3,000 French Jews were arrested from his area alone and transferred to the concentration camp at DRANCY.

Barbie, nicknamed "The Butcher of Lyon," was particularly zealous and fanatical. He not only ordered torture but applied it himself. He was behind many mass executions, and commanded the DEPORTATION of 842 people from Lyon, both Jews and members of the French Resistance. He ordered the deaths of 44 Jewish children between the ages of 3 and 13—children who had found refuge in a group home. He tortured to death the celebrated French Resistance leader, Jean Moulin.

When the war ended, Barbie was employed by the United States as a secret agent in GERMANY. He moved to Bolivia in 1951 and became a Bolivian

Klaus Barbie in uniform during the war

citizen under a false name. Despite his disappearance, he was tried for war crimes in France in 1952 and again in 1954. Both times he was sentenced to death.

In 1972, French Nazi-hunter Serge Klarsfeld discovered that Barbie was living in South America. He remained there under the protection of the Bolivian government until he was finally extradited to France in 1983. A telegram he had sent announcing the murder of the children in the group home was used as evidence against him. In addition, witnesses who had been Barbie's victims gave detailed testimony about his cruelty. He was convicted of crimes against humanity and sentenced to life imprisonment, the maximum punishment allowed by French law. He died in jail.

BAUM GRUPPE

SEE YOUTH MOVEMENTS.

BEER HALL PUTSCH

see HITLER, ADOLF.

BEIT LOHAMEI HA-GETTAOT

see GHETTO FIGHTERS' HOUSE.

B E L G I U M

Country in western Europe that was invaded by the German army on 10 May 1940, and surrendered on 28 May. Its king, Leopold III, remained in Belgium. However, the prime minister and most other minis-

ters fled and established a government-in-exile in London. The Germans imposed a military administration on Belgium and annexed two districts of northern FRANCE.

On the eve of occupation, about 79,000 Jews lived in Belgium, the majority in Brussels and Antwerp. Most Jews were recently arrived immigrants from eastern European countries and GERMANY. Less than 10 percent were Belgian citizens. Several thousand Jews managed to flee the country, mainly during the invasion. Of those who remained, 34,801 were rounded up and deported, most of them to AUSCHWITZ. In all, 28,902 died.

Anti-Jewish policies in Belgium were similar to

Belgians running away from the Germans

those in other Nazi-occupied countries, but they were set in motion at a slower pace. The policies included removing Jews from government positions and the professions, confiscating their businesses and property, confining them to the four main cities (Brussels, Antwerp, Liège, and Charleroi), imposing night curfews, and requiring them to wear the yellow BADGE. This was followed by FORCED LABOR and finally DEPORTATIONS (beginning in August 1942).

Not all Belgian citizens felt the same about the fate of the Jews. Some collaborated with the Nazis. On the other hand, many worked to save Jews. These efforts were connected to anti-German feelings, a deep commitment to democracy, or the influence of socialism and communism. During the deportation period, close to 25,000 Jews found hiding places, many with the aid of Belgian underground movements and some Catholic leaders.

During the first year of occupation, the influence of Zionists groups grew. The Association of Jews in Belgium (AJB) was established as a kind of JUDENRAT in November 1941, under the leadership of Chief Rabbi Salomon Ullman. All Jewish organizations were supposed to work through the AJB. Soon, there was resistance from some Jewish groups, mainly leftist, to both the Germans and the policies of the AJB. This resistance led to the establishment

of the illegal Committee of Defense of Jews in Belgium (CDJ) when the deportations started. It was supported by the Communist Independence Front. It helped to find hiding places for 4,000 children and it assisted a group of 571 Jews who succeeded in escaping from trains bound for Auschwitz. The most notable escape took place on 19–20 April 1943, when 231 Jews jumped from a train. Seventeen of them were helped by a resistance group; 23 were killed by the German guards. The fact that over half the Belgian Jewish community survived the Holocaust is largely due to the efforts of the Jews themselves.

BELORUSSIA (BELARUS)

see BYELORUSSIA.

B E L Z E C

DEATH CAMP located in southeastern POLAND in the LUBLIN district, alongside a main railway line. Between March and December 1942, Belzec served as a German extermination center, at which between 550,000 and 600,000 Jews were killed.

It was originally established in 1940 as a slave labor camp. Its Jewish prisoners dug anti-tank ditches and built fortifications against a possible Soviet invasion. Belzec became part of the German killing system on 17 March 1942. Barbed wire surrounded the 886-square foot death camp. Watchtowers were located at the corners. The entrance was through a gate wide enough to admit a train.

During the first four weeks of its operation, some 80,000 Jews were murdered—30,000 from LVOV and half that number from Lublin. The German staff of Belzec was headed by Christian Wirth who was assisted by Franz STANGL. Both were experienced killers who began their careers in the EUTHANASIA PROGRAM. They were assisted by Ukrainian prisoners of war. Some 700 to 1,000 Jewish prisoners were kept alive to help with the killing.

The killing process resembled an assembly line. Jews were deported (see DEPORTATIONS) from the GHETTOS by train. When they arrived, their possessions were confiscated and they were forced to undress. Women's hair was cut. The entire group of prisoners would be gassed in one of the three GAS

CHAMBERS at Belzec and their bodies buried in pits. At first, the killing would take several hours, but after larger gas chambers were built, it took less than two hours. The materials taken from the victims were then sorted and packaged.

Before the camp was closed, the Germans tried to destroy all evidence of murder. They opened the mass graves, removed the bodies and burned them (see AKTION 1005). By December 1942, Belzec's operations were complete; the Jews of the Generalgouvernement area (German-occupied Poland) were murdered and the last of Belzec's prisoners were sent to SOBIBÓR to be killed.

BEN-GURION, DAVID

(1886–1973) Zionist leader and first Prime Minister of the State of Israel. From 1935 to 1948, David Ben-Gurion served as chairman of the JEWISH AGENCY. In 1935, he proposed a rescue program that would bring a million European Jewish immigrants to Palestine over the course of 20 years, but this could not be implemented. As conditions for Jews in Europe worsened, his desire to bring about mass immigration became increasingly intense. However, the British WHITE PAPER OF 1939, which severely limited Jewish immigration to Palestine, blocked his plans. In 1939, he responded to the White Paper by calling for an "immigration war"—bringing Jews to Palestine "illegally" behind the backs of the British.

When WORLD WAR II broke out, his supreme goal became the defeat of the Nazis. He said that he would "combat the anti-Zionist White Paper as though there were no war; and fight against the

---

I come to you with empty pockets. I have no immigration certificates for you. I can only tell you that you are not abandoned. You are not alone. You will not live endlessly in camps like this. All of you who want to come to Palestine will be brought there as soon as it is humanly possible. I bring you no certificates—only hope.

David Ben-Gurion addressing
Holocaust survivors in a displaced
persons camp in Europe after the war

David Ben-Gurion visited a displaced persons' camp in Germany. This account is by Rabbi Judah Nadich, a U.S. army chaplain, who accompanied him on the visit.

Suddenly, one of the Jews in the group happened to peer into the automobile and, recognizing the strong face and white shock of hair, suddenly screamed in an unearthly voice, "Ben-Gurion! Ben-Gurion!"

Like one man, the entire group turned toward the car and began shrieking, shouting the name of the man who was accepted by all of them as their own political leader. But he was far more than that to them. He was the personal embodiment of all their hopes for the future. During all the many years of their hell, during what had seemed like several lifetimes of subjection to Nazi debasement and degradation, that which had kept them alive, that which had buoyed them up even amidst the darkest days, was the yearning the longing, the hope for Palestine.

Now, after all these many years, here was Palestine right in the midst of their displaced persons camp on German soil! For who better than Ben-Gurion personified Eretz Yisrael, the Land of Israel, and its fight for freedom and independence?

As Ben-Gurion entered the hall, the people spontaneously burst into the Zionist anthem, Hatikvah, the hope that had never died. As he stood on the platform before them, the people broke forth into cheers, into song and, finally, into weeping. At last he began to speak, his voice choked up, his eyes filled. He had to stop as he broke down for a moment. In the sudden quiet one could hear the muffled sobbing from all sides of the auditorium. Very few eyes were dry. For the incredible was true; the impossible had happened. Ben-Gurion was in their midst and they had lived despite Hitler.

Germans on the side of Britain as though there were no White Paper." He pressed for the all-out mobilization of the Jews of Palestine for the war effort and for forming Jewish units in the British army. He saw the establishment of a Jewish state as the goal of Zionist policy, and was the architect of the policy document of the Zionist movement in 1942, which called for the establishment of a Jewish state in Palestine after the war. This view guided all his political actions until 1948, when his policies were put into action and he declared the independence of the Jewish State of Israel.

BENOÎT, MARIE

(1895–1987) French Catholic monk active in rescuing Jews. He lived in the Capuchin monastery in Marseilles, FRANCE.

In 1942, the VICHY government of occupied France actively participated in rounding up Jews for deportation. Benoît devoted himself to helping Jews escape to safety in SPAIN or SWITZERLAND. Coordinating with various Christian and Jewish organizations, he provided documents and help with passage to Jews who would have otherwise been trapped. After he was transferred to work inside the Vatican he was

Father Marie Benoît, 1984

instrumental in helping Jews in Rome, Italy and the surrounding area. He also tried to organize a massive rescue of the 30,000 Jews of Nice, France but this plan ultimately failed. Benoît was hunted by the GESTAPO and escaped arrest several times. After the liberation of Rome, he was honored by the Italian Jewish community. He was decorated by France, and in 1966 Israel honored him with the title "Righteous Among the Nations."

BERGEN-BELSEN

Nazi CONCENTRATION CAMP in northwest GERMANY. In May 1943, a SOVIET PRISONERS OF WAR camp was taken over by the SS and renamed a "detention camp." It was to house a special group of Jews whom the Nazis thought could be used in exchange deals with the Allies. These "exchange Jews" included people with important political or economic connections abroad and those who held South American passports or entry papers to PALESTINE. They began to arrive in Belsen in July 1943.

The Belsen detention camp was divided into several sub-camps for different types of prisoners. Each group was kept in separate compounds and subject to different rules. These groups included Jews with passports from neutral countries, Polish Jews with South American papers, a group of 4,000 Dutch Jews from WESTERBORK, and a transport of Hungarian Jews, whom Heinrich HIMMLER hoped to exchange for money and goods. In fact, very few of the "exchange-Jews" were actually exchanged.

Although food was insufficient and some prisoners had to endure FORCED LABOR, conditions in Belsen during its first 10 months were better than in other Nazi CAMPS. During 1944, however, Belsen gradually became more like a "typical" concentration camp. Conditions worsened seriously. It became a dumping site for prisoners from other camps. In March 1944, one section of Belsen was named a "recuperation camp" and received ill and exhausted slave laborers from DORA-MITTELBAU. No attempt was made by the camp authorities to make them well, however. Many suffered and died in terrible conditions.

As the Russian army advanced into POLAND in 1944, the Nazis began to move prisoners and slave laborers into German camps. Some were taken in open trucks in freezing weather with very little food or water. Many were marched on foot. In the summer of 1944, these transports began to arrive in Belsen. They included thousands of women from AUSCHWITZ. During the winter of 1944–1945, the overcrowding and lack of sanitary facilities and food supplies caused many deaths. In December 1944, Josef KRAMER was appointed camp commandant. He officially made Belsen into a tougher concentration camp.

When the camp was liberated by the British on 15 April 1945, the horrified soldiers found 60,000 starved and diseased prisoners. More than half of them were Jews. Over 10,000 unburied and decomposing corpses lay around the camp. People continued to die for weeks after the liberation.

Eleven of the staff at Bergen-Belsen, including Kramer, were sentenced to death by a British military court in November 1945. They were executed on 12 December 1945. The British burned down the barracks of the main camp. Part of the site was used as a DISPLACED PERSONS camp until 1951.

The site of the main camp at Bergen-Belsen is a memorial open to the public. The mass graves are marked with simple plaques estimating the number of people buried there. No buildings remain; as a measure to prevent the spread of typhus, the wooden huts that housed the prisoners were burned down by soldier of the British liberating army.

The first memorial to be erected on the site, in 1945, was a large cross. A Jewish stone memorial was unveiled in April 1946 and in 1947, work began on an international memorial wall and obelisk. A visitors' center opened in 1966 and was completely redeveloped in the late 1980s. A permanent exhibition documenting the history of the Nazi regime and the Bergen-Belsen camp was opened in 1990.

BERGSON GROUP

A group belonging to the nationalist Revisionist Zionist movement, active in various Zionist and Jewish causes in the United States between 1939 and 1948. It was headed by the Palestinian Jew, Hillel Kook, who used the name Peter Bergson in the United States .

During World War II, the group's activities were aimed at raising a Jewish army and rescuing Jews from Europe. Its policies were often opposed by those of the official Zionist movement, since the Bergson Group advocated more activism. A number of Jews from PALESTINE and the United States participated in the group.

The Bergson Group created various organizations, including the American Friends of a Jewish

Surviving prisoners of Bergen-Belsen upon the arrival of the British liberators

Palestine (1939–1941) which supported "illegal" immigration to Palestine; the Committee for a Jewish Army (1941–1943); and, after the killing of European Jewry became known, the Emergency Committee to Rescue the Jews of Europe (1943–1945).

BERIHA ("ESCAPE" or "FLIGHT")

Hebrew term for the postwar flight of Holocaust survivors from POLAND to GERMANY, AUSTRIA, and ITALY en route to PALESTINE. Its aim was to help survivors reach the Mediterranean and Black Sea coasts, where they could board ships of the ALIYA BET organization for the journey to Palestine.

Jewish REFUGEES began to flee Eastern Europe in 1944 as the German army withdrew. This increased in 1946 because of antisemitic violence in these countries. As a movement, Beriha was led at first by former PARTISAN leaders, including Abba KOVNER and Yizhak ZUCKERMAN. It became more formally organized with the help of Jews sent from Palestine and by Zionist youth movements.

Most of these refugees ended up in Italy, although a few also reached the Black Sea ports of Varna (Bulgaria) or Constanta (Romania). In 1945 and the first half of 1946, they were escorted to Italy by members of the JEWISH BRIGADE. Thousands of liberated Jewish CONCENTRATION CAMP survivors in Germany and Austria were also taken from their miser-

able camp environments in small groups. They were brought secretly across borders. After being temporarily housed in shelters near the Italian border, they were smuggled into Italy with groups of Italian prisoners of war who were returning from SOVIET RUSSIA. Once in Italy, they were moved south to wait for boats to Palestine. At this time, the British were blockading the shores of Palestine to prevent the entrance of unauthorized immigrants. Those ships that escaped detection landed the Jews secretly in Palestine. Those caught by the British were sent to detention camps in CYPRUS. Beriha was aided by Jews in Europe and, behind the scenes, by a number of European governments.

B E R L I N

Capital of GERMANY. In 1933, one third of Germany's Jewish population (160,564) lived in Berlin. The Jewish community faced many challenges as the Nazis rose to power. Since Jewish students were excluded from non-Jewish schools, the community had to provide education for them. As Jews were increasingly fired from their jobs, the community had to expand its social welfare system. Its most important task, however, was to organize emigration. Some 50,000 Berlin Jews managed to leave Germany by the end of 1937.

Berlin Jews experienced all the Nazis' discrimina-

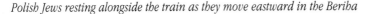

Polish Jews resting alongside the train as they move eastward in the Beriha

tions and anti-Jewish measures (see NUREMBERG LAWS). In addition, local police and officials in Berlin had their own anti-Jewish policies. Most of Berlin's synagogues were destroyed during KRISTALLNACHT (November 1938), when 12,000 Jewish men were imprisoned in the SACHSENHAUSEN CONCENTRATION CAMP.

The number of Jewish-owned stores dropped from over 6,000 in 1933 to 3,105 in April 1938. By the end of 1938, the remaining stores owned by Jews were either closed or "Aryanized" (see ARYANIZATION). In December 1938, the Berlin police prohibited Jews from attending theaters, concerts, museums, and sports arenas. Jews were also banned from some streets in the government district. In 1938 and the first half of 1939, more than 30,000 Berlin Jews left Germany. By summer 1940, 73,327 Jews remained in Berlin. In July 1941, approximately 27,000 Jews were recruited for FORCED LABOR.

The first DEPORTATIONS of Jews from Berlin took place on 18 October 1941 for the LÓDZ ghetto. In June 1942, the elderly, war veterans, and other "privileged" groups were sent to THERESIENSTADT. From November 1942, all deportations from Berlin to POLAND were sent to AUSCHWITZ.

Although Josef GOEBBELS declared Berlin *judenrein* ("free of Jews") in May 1943, there were approximately 4,700 Jews left there at the time of its liberation. Most of these had been protected by non-Jewish spouses or had one non-Jewish parent. In addition, 1,900 Jews returned from Theresienstadt and other CONCENTRATION CAMPS, and about 1,400 hid and survived the war. More than 55,000 Berlin Jews were victims of the Holocaust.

BERMUDA CONFERENCE

Conference convened on 19 April 1943, as the result of growing public pressure in GREAT BRITAIN and the United States to find a solution for the European REFUGEE problem. Late in 1942 reports began to

Adolf Hitler passing the Brandenburg Gate on his way to the opening ceremonies of the Berlin Olympic Games, 1936

> The Bermuda Conference was wholly ineffective, as I view it, and we knew it would be....
>
> From Memorandum, Myron Taylor, Chairman of Evian Conference, to Secretary of State Cordell Hull, 30 April 1943.

circulate outside GERMANY confirming Nazi efforts to exterminate the Jews. Public demands for rescue action mounted among the various Jewish humanitarian organizations. The British Foreign Office called on the United States State Department to consult jointly on what could be done. The conference took place in Bermuda.

Several factors indicate that the Bermuda Conference was actually planned to calm public opinion, but not to address seriously the problem of refugees. The location is the first factor. Canada had objected to Ottawa as a site for the conference, and the U.S. State Department rejected Washington. Both of these locations would have afforded wider press coverage and direct access by humanitarian organizations. Bermuda was chosen and the number of reporters allowed was limited to five. Humanitarian agencies, such as the AMERICAN JEWISH JOINT DISTRIBUTION COMMITTEE, were not allowed to attend.

A further factor which limited the conference's power to deal with the humanitarian issue at hand was the absence of high-ranking representatives in the American delegation. Leaders of significant Jewish organizations were excluded.

The problem of refugees in general and not the uniquely Jewish focus of the Nazi genocide was on the agenda. Even the memoranda from the Jewish groups were not allowed to refer to the problem of European Jewry. Consequently, from the outset, the conference was limited in its ability to deal decisively with the mass murder of Jews by the Nazis.

The proceedings were kept secret and by December 1943, when the final report was published, it was condemned as a pretext. The Bermuda Conference failed to save even a single victim. The Allied countries were almost completely unwilling to depart from their immigration quotas to address the problem of the European Jewry.

BERNADOTTE, FOLKE

(1895–1948) Swedish count, diplomat and representative of the Swedish Red Cross.

During the spring of 1945, as the war was drawing to its close, Bernadotte was able to negotiate the exchange of 7,000 Scandinavian citizens being held in German CONCENTRATION CAMPS. Among those released were 400 Danish Jews imprisoned at THERESIENSTADT. In a later negotiation, he was able to free several thousand Jewish women who were being held at RAVENSBRÜCK. They were then brought to SWEDEN.

In the final days of the war, Heinrich HIMMLER met with Bernadotte to try to negotiate terms for a German surrender. Himmler gave Bernadotte a letter to carry to General Dwight D. EISENHOWER. It said that GERMANY was willing to surrender to the Allies in the west, if it could continue the war in Russia. Bernadotte informed Himmler, on 27 April 1945, that the Allies had rejected his terms.

On 20 May 1948, Bernadotte was appointed by the United Nations Security Council as a special negotiator in the Arab-Israel conflict. He successfully arranged a truce. The truce lost public support,

Count Folke Bernadotte

however, since the land settlement plan was very different from the plan that had been suggested by the United Nations. On 17 September 1948, Bernadotte was assassinated in Jerusalem by unknown attackers believed to have been connected with Lechi, the most extreme of the Israel underground paramilitary groups.

B E S S A R A B I A

Region of eastern Europe. ROMANIA received Bessarabia from Russia after World War I and ruled it until 1940. At that time, it was taken over by SOVIET RUSSIA under the NAZI-SOVIET PACT. However, after GERMANY invaded Russia in 1941, the troops of Romania—now an ally of Germany—retook Bessarabia. The Romanian dictator, Ion ANTONESCU, proclaimed the Jews an "enemy population" and ordered the area "cleansed." This meant killing all Jews living in villages and concentrating all Jews living in towns into GHETTOS. The Romanians established a special unit to kill Jews, which worked closely with German EINSATZGRUPPEN (killing units). The Romanians were even more fanatical in killing Jews than the Germans. An Einsatzgruppen report criticized them for too much looting and for not burying those they executed. Of the 200,000 Jews who had lived in Bessarabia before the war, only 126,000 remained in September 1941. Many had fled. Some had bought baptism certificates to save themselves, and others had been killed or died from starvation and epidemics.

In August 1941, German and Romanian military staffs established the TRANSNISTRIA area in part of the UKRAINE occupied by the Romanians. Here, surviving Jews were sent from Bessarabia and BUKOVINA. About half of the Bessarabian Jews sent to Transnistria were killed. The rest were put into FORCED LABOR

Jews deported from Bessarabia on their way to forced labor camps, 1941

CAMPS. By mid-1942, only a couple of hundred Jews remained in Bessarabia. In August 1944, Bessarabia was liberated by Soviet forces, and was made part of Soviet Russia.

BEST, WERNER

(1903–) Senior member of the SS, and German plenipotentiary in DENMARK from 1942 to 1945. Best was a lawyer by training, and in 1929 became a judge. He joined the NAZI PARTY in 1930, and the SS the following year. He served as legal advisor to the GESTAPO and was a close collaborator of Reinhard HEYDRICH. He served for two years (1940–1942) in occupied FRANCE. In November 1942, he was sent to Denmark.

It is not completely clear what role he played in the DEPORTATIONS, political murders, and suppression of the resistance in areas that were under his rule. However, the special success of the rescue of Danish Jewry supports the view that he did not follow the usual Nazi policies. Some evidence connected Best to a meeting in which Adolf HITLER ordered revenge murders in Denmark because of sabotage. Other reports speak of a conversation in which the Nazi foreign minister Joachim von RIBBENTROP accused Best of failure to deal brutally with saboteurs.

Werner Best

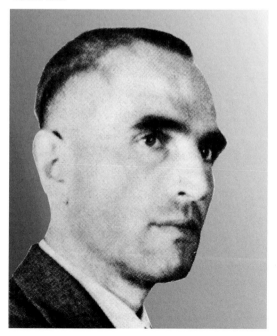

In any event, in 1948, a Danish court sentenced him to death. This sentence was then changed to imprisonment and Best was released in 1951. He was arrested again in 1969 for involvement in mass murder in POLAND, but was released for health reasons in 1972—although in fact he lived to an old age. He returned to civilian life in GERMANY in the legal profession.

BIALYSTOK

City in northeastern POLAND. Before WORLD WAR II, Bialystok had a population of 50,000 Jews, almost half the population of the city. An additional 350,000 Jews lived in outlying districts. Jews were particularly active in the city's textile industry.

After the Germans invaded Poland in September 1939, they handed over the city to the Russian government (see NAZI-SOVIET PACT). On 27 June 1941, after the Germans attacked SOVIET RUSSIA, they drove out the Russians and the following day, the Germans destroyed the Jewish quarter. Over the next few weeks, thousands of Jews were murdered by the EINSATZGRUPPEN (killing groups). At this time, a Jewish council, or JUDENRAT, was also organized. The chief rabbi, Rabbi Gedaliah Rosenbaum, was the head of the council, but its real leader was his deputy, Ephraim BARASCH.

On 1 August 1941, 50,000 Jews were herded into a small closed GHETTO. Workers from the ghetto were forced to make weapons and textiles for the Germans. All Jews between the ages of 15 and 65 worked in exchange for small amounts of bread. These rations were later reduced to almost nothing.

On 5 February 1943, the Germans began the liquidation of the ghetto. One thousand weak or sick Jews were killed and thousands were sent to their deaths at TREBLINKA. The final destruction of the ghetto began on 16 August 1943.

In the ghetto, an underground Jewish RESISTANCE movement had formed. It was led by Mordechai TENENBAUM, who was sent by the JEWISH FIGHTING ORGANIZATION of WARSAW. The movement suffered from lack of arms, organization and support from other movements. When the Germans began the liquidation of the ghetto, the underground was unprepared. Within the next few months, however, three groups fled to the forests where they mounted attacks against the overwhelmingly superior German forces.

On 16 August 1943, the Jewish underground began an attack on the Germans. After the first day of fighting, 72 men retreated to a bunker. Within days the Germans found them and shot and killed all except one. Over 100 more fighters escaped and joined outside resistance groups. By September 1943, 40,000 Jews remaining in Bialystok were deported to Treblinka and MAJDANEK. The remaining members of the underground formed a single group called Kadimah (Hebrew for "Onward"). They joined a group of Soviet parachutists toward the end of the year. At end of the war, only 200 Jews from Bialystok had survived in the CONCENTRATION CAMPS.

BIEBOW, HANS

(1902–1947) Head of the Nazi administration in the LÓDZ ghetto. Biebow took advantage of the cheap labor in the ghetto to make himself rich. Unlike some of the other GHETTOS, the workers of which had to leave to reach their places of work, Lódz was completely closed. All industry there was completely under the control of Biebow and his 250-person administrative staff. He set up factories in the ghetto that exploited the trapped residents. He also stole their property. When the order came to liquidate the Lódz ghetto in August 1944, he was involved in deporting Jews to their deaths at CHELMNO and AUSCHWITZ. Biebow was tried by the Poles following the war and executed in 1947.

BIELSKI, TUVIA

(1906–1987) Jewish RESISTANCE commander who, with his three brothers, Zusya, Asael and Aharon, established a FAMILY CAMP in a forest in BYELORUSSIA (Belorus) consisting of more than 1,200 Jews—men, women, and children, old and young. They showed that resistance and rescue could be combined.

When the Germans arrived in the ghetto of Novogrudok in Byelorussia, they murdered Bielski's parents and others in his family. Tuvia and his brothers

Hans Biebow (right), head of the German administration in Lodz Ghetto, talking to Mordechai Chaim Rumkowski, Chairman of the Jewish Council

Tuvia Bielski

escaped to the nearby Naliboki Forest. They sent a message to the ghetto: "organize as many friends and acquaintances as possible. Send them to us in the woods. We will be waiting for you." Slowly, over the next two years, 1,200 Jews took to the forest rather than wait for DEPORTATION.

The Bielski brothers obtained weapons and formed a PARTISAN unit, with Tuvia as its commander. They stole food and took revenge on Byelorussian police and local farmers who had murdered Jews. Conditions in the ghetto worsened and the Bielskis' reputation grew. More Jews joined the Bielski camp. Frustrated by their unsuccessful efforts to arrest Tuvia, the Germans offered 100,000 marks for his capture.

Unlike other partisan units, which consisted only of the young and the able bodied, Bielski accepted all Jews. He ignored orders from Soviet partisan commanders to let in fighting forces only, since this would have abandoned women, children, and the elderly to certain death.

In the summer of 1944, after the region had been liberated, the Bielski brothers and the 1,230 Jews who had been with them, returned to Novogrudok. They had survived as a group.

In late 1944, Asael Bielski was killed in battle as a Soviet soldier. After the war, Tuvia returned to Poland and then moved to Palestine. He emigrated to the United States in 1954, with Zusya and Aharon and their families.

B I R K E N A U

see AUSCHWITZ.

B L I T Z K R I E G

German for "lightning war." Beginning in 1939, this became an important element of Germany's military strategy at the beginning of WORLD WAR II. Blitzkrieg strategy used aerial bombings and fast large-scale offensive maneuvers planned to catch the enemy off guard and to win a quick victory. As a result, major parts of POLAND fell to GERMANY within a few days, and the entire country was conquered in a week. Germany also used this tactic against DENMARK, NORWAY, YUGOSLAVIA, GREECE, FRANCE, BELGIUM and the NETHERLANDS. Each was overrun by the Nazis in a matter of days or weeks.

B L O B E L ,   P A U L

(1894–1951) SS officer and commander of a sub-group of one of the EINSATZGRUPPEN (killing groups). Blobel joined the Nazi Party in 1931. He enlisted in the SS in January 1932 and by January 1941 had risen to the rank of colonel in the SD, the security service of the SS. In June 1942, he was appointed commander of a sub-unit of Einsatzgruppe C, which operated in the UKRAINE. Tens of thousands of murders were committed under his command. The most notorious was the shooting of 33,771 Jews from KIEV into a ravine called BABI YAR in September 1941. Later in the war, Blobel was appointed leader of AKTION 1005, an operation aimed at destroying all traces of the mass murders. Blobel was sentenced to death by the Nuremberg Military Tribunal (see TRIALS OF WAR CRIMINALS) in 1948, and was hanged.

Paul Blobel

B L U M ,   L É O N

(1872–1950) French socialist politician. Blum was a committed Jew, a lawyer and a successful author. He became one of FRANCE's most important socialist politicians in the first half of the 20th century.

In the 1930s, Blum was a key organizer of a leftist coalition of parties, including the Communist Party. It was called the Popular Front. In 1936, this coalition won a majority in parliament. Thus, Blum became

> The men of Vichy failed to break Léon Blum's spirit. After months of imprisonment he never weakened in his faith in the victory of civilization over barbarism, or in his hope in the final victory of socialism. The last message I received from him just before he was taken to Germany breathed the same triumphant spirit. There was no word of his personal sufferings and danger. His whole thoughts were devoted to plans for the future of the world, when victory would be won and civilization saved. His enemies may enslave his body; they cannot enslave his soul.
>
> Clement Attlee on Léon Blum, 1943

Léon Blum

prime minister, the first Jew in France to hold this position.

France's conservative political leaders strongly opposed the Popular Front's policies of anti-FASCISM and their inclusion of communists in the government. Blum became the key target of this political anger. This was partly because the opponents focused on Blum's Jewishness to gain the support of antisemites.

When the pro-Nazi VICHY regime came to power in 1940, its leaders increased their attacks on Blum. They blamed him for France's being unprepared for the German invasion. The Vichy regime brought charges of "war guilt" against him in 1942. Since Blum was trained as a lawyer, his courtroom defense was far superior to the performance of his accusers. The trial had to be discontinued.

Blum was sent to BUCHENWALD in 1943, and was transferred to DACHAU shortly before the war's end. After the war, he returned to active political life, and briefly served again as premier.

BOHEMIA AND MORAVIA

Western region of CZECHOSLOVAKIA. On 15 March 1939, Nazi Germany occupied the area and made it a German protectorate. This brought an additional 120,000 Jews under Hitler's rule, including 17,000 who had fled from the Sudetenland (see CZECHOSLOVAKIA) after its occupation.

Immediately following the occupation, a wave of Jew-baiting and arrests was initiated by FASCIST organizations. Synagogues were burned and Jews attacked on the streets and rounded up. In June 1939, a decree was issued banning Jews from almost all economic activity in the country. Jewish property was seized. It is estimated that the equivalent of half a billion dollars was stolen in this manner.

During this period, the GESTAPO was busy issuing exit permits in order to receive cash payments and

Kurt Dalvege, Nazi Governor of Bohemia and Moravia, testifying at his trial in Prague

to seize the property of the emigrés. Hence, through the HAAVARAH Agreement between the Czech Ministry of Finance and the Jewish Agency, 2,000 Czech Jews reached PALESTINE. In a similar arrangement, the YOUTH ALIYA and other movements arranged for many youth to be transferred to western Europe for agricultural training. Over 26,600 Czech Jews were able to escape to GREAT BRITAIN, the United States, Palestine and South America before emigration was banned in 1941.

In June 1939, Adolf EICHMANN arrived in PRAGUE and established an office to promote Jewish emigration. With the outbreak of war in September 1939, a reign of terror began. Jews were dismissed from their jobs and banned from many pulbic places. Food was rationed, Jewish children were expelled from schools, curfews were imposed and Jews were ordered to wear yellow stars. The Jews' economic situation was so poor that the Prague community could not even maintain its soup kitchen. In October, 1,000 members of the community were sent to NISKO, and then marched to LUBLIN. Many of the survivors managed to return home with news of the horror of their treatment.

Czechoslovak patriotism increased, as a response to Reinhard HEYDRICH's reign of terror. Following a mass student rally, over 1,000 Czechs were sent to CONCENTRATION CAMPS and all institutions of higher learning were closed. This caused some change in the feelings of many Czechs toward their fellow Jewish citizens: sympathy toward the Jews became one expression of Czech hatred of foreign rule. However, the acceptance of Jewish disappearance seems to have been the norm among the Czech population. The Nazi transportations of Jews to LÓDZ and the establishment of the THERESIENSTADT ghetto near Prague served two purposes: to remove Jews from the society, and to serve as a warning to other Czechs who would challenge Nazi rule. In 1941, Theresienstadt became a transit camp for Jews on their way to AUSCHWITZ. In 1942 alone, 55,000 Jews were sent from the Protectorate of Bohemia and Moravia to Theresienstadt. Most of them were sent on to the death camps. Before the deportations started, 92,000 Jews were living in the Protectorate—14,000 survived.

The Nazis showed particular interest in the cultural and religious articles they had confiscated from Jews. They collected vast numbers of Torah scrolls and all other Jewish religious items in order to create what was planned as "The Central Museum of the Extinguished Jewish Race" in Prague. Ironically, in their attempt to celebrate Jewish annihilation, the Nazis amassed and preserved one of the largest and most valuable Judaica collections in Europe. The collection is now housed in a number of synagogues in Prague's Jewish Quarter.

BONHOEFFER, DIETRICH

(1906–1945) German theologian. Bonhoeffer was a minister in the Confessing Church, a group of German Protestants who opposed Nazi policies. Bonhoeffer was more radical than most Confessing Christians, since he believed that active political resistance should be taken against the Nazi evil.

In 1940, he began to work for German military intelligence, supposedly gathering information on foreign Churches. In reality, he used his contacts with other clergymen to send messages about what was happening in GERMANY. He sent the first report about the October 1941 DEPORTATIONS of BERLIN Jews to foreign Christian leaders. They passed it on to the United States State Department. He also tried to win foreign support for the German PLOT TO KILL HITLER.

Bonhoeffer was arrested in April 1943. After the attempted assassination of Adolf HITLER in July 1944, the GESTAPO discovered papers linking Bonhoeffer and other members of in his family to the plot. He was hanged on 9 April 1945, at the CONCENTRATION CAMP in Flossenberg.

BOOK BURNING

Nazi practice that was begun in order to show their contempt for Jewish culture. Upon gaining power in GERMANY in 1933, the Nazis began burning Bibles, prayer books, and other traditional Jewish works. They also destroyed the works of Jewish, and some non-Jewish, poets, writers and thinkers, who they felt were "corrupting" ARYAN Germanic culture. These acts were inspired by the Nazi leadership, but were made to look like the spontaneous action of students and the SA in most major cities, especially those with universities. Josef GOEBBELS organized a

Hitler Youth burning books written by Jews

Martin Bormann

mass burning of "Jewish" books on 10 May 1933. As the Germans advanced in Europe, they continued to burn books. In Kalisz, POLAND, the biblical scrolls from the synagogues were burned. In PRAGUE it was estimated that millions of books by Jewish authors were burned. The prophecy of the German poet Heinrich Heine, "Where they burn books, there they will burn people," was fulfilled in Nazi-occupied Europe.

BORMANN, MARTIN

(1900–1945) Nazi leader and a key planner of the HOLOCAUST.

Bormann joined the NAZI PARTY in 1927. He rose steadily through the ranks to become head of Rudolf HESS's office. There he administrated Adolf HITLER's personal finances. Hitler called him "the most loyal of comrades." In 1935, he was appointed deputy minister of CHURCHES. Bormann was strongly against Christianity, which he saw as the opposite of Nazism. In 1941, when Hess flew to Scotland and did not return, Bormann was appointed a minister and took over most of Hess's functions. He was now extremely powerful, especially after he became Hitler's secretary in 1942. According to the decree of 24 January 1942, Bormann was given authority over the laws and commands of the "FINAL SOLUTION." He co-signed the decree of July 1943, which placed Jews under the control of the GESTAPO. Immoral and sadistic, Bormann was centrally involved in planning the mass-murder of European Jewry. He was with Hitler until Hitler's suicide.

For years after the war, there were rumors that Bormann had escaped to South America. At the TRIALS OF WAR CRIMINALS at Nuremberg, he was tried in absentia and sentenced to death. However, it is now generally accepted that he died in Berlin a few days after Hitler's death, during the Soviet bombardment of that city.

BOROWSKI, TADEUSZ

(1922–1951) Non-Jewish Polish writer and concentration camp survivor.

Borowski was born in Zhitomir in the Soviet UKRAINE to Polish parents. His father was imprisoned by the Soviets and after his release, the family returned to WARSAW. Borowski showed early talent as a writer.

When the Germans occupied POLAND, only Nazi publications were permitted to be issued. Borowski published some of his anti-Nazi writings secretly

---

If I had said to you as we danced together in my room in the light of the paraffin lamp: listen, take a million people, or two million, or three, kill them in such a way that no one knows about it, not even they themselves, enslave several hundred thousand more, destroy their mutual loyalty, pit man against man, surely you would have thought me mad. Except that I would probably not have said these things to you. I would not have wanted to spoil our mood.

from "Auschwitz, Our Home (A Letter)" in Tadeusz Borowski's "This Way for the Gas, Ladies and Gentlemen"

---

and was arrested by the Nazis. He was imprisoned in AUSCHWITZ and DACHAU from April 1943 to May 1945, when he was liberated. He was one of the most promising postwar Polish writers. Among his writings are first-hand accounts of life in Auschwitz, and his widely-read collection, *This Way for the Gas, Ladies and Gentlemen*. He committed suicide in 1951.

BOUSQUET, RENÉ

(?–1993) Secretary-general of the VICHY police from April 1942 until the end of 1943. Bousquet was responsible for the DEPORTATION of some 30,000 Jews from both occupied FRANCE and the southern unoccupied zone.

Bousquet was an enthusiastic official of the Vichy government. Under his administration, 13,000 Jews were rounded up by French police in PARIS on 16 July 1942, and deported to their deaths. Bousquet suggested to Adolf EICHMANN, during Eichmann's visit to Paris in July 1942, that foreign Jews living in the unoccupied zone of France should also be deported.

In 1949, Bousquet was cleared of charges of treason, but found guilty of "national shame." He was stripped of his rights as a citizen for five years. In the years that followed, he lived a carefree and prosperous life in Paris. In 1989, he was charged with CRIMES AGAINST HUMANITY, because of his direct responsibility for the deportation of non-French Jews, including children, from both occupied and unoccupied France. In June 1993, before the trial started, Bousquet was shot dead by an assassin.

BOYCOTT, ANTI-JEWISH

The first official Nazi attack on German Jewry. This one-day boycott of all Jewish shops and businesses in GERMANY was planned by the Nazi leaders. Julius STREICHER was responsible for the organization of the boycott. It began at 10.00 A.M. on 1 April 1933.

The Nazis had created a group called the Central Committee for Defense Against Jewish Atrocity and Boycott Propaganda. Jews were labeled the enemy of Germany by the Nazis and were accused of trying to discredit the THIRD REICH abroad. Josef GOEBBELS announced that the boycott was needed as punishment against this "Jewish atrocity propaganda." The Central Committee issued instructions to all SA units as to how to enforce the boycott. On the day of the action, uniformed SA men were posted outside Jewish businesses all over Germany. They urged "German people" not to enter. Yellow Stars of David were painted on shop windows to identify the Jewish stores. Posters were put up carrying antisemitic caricatures and slogans, like "The Jews of the World are Trying to Destroy Germany" and "Don't Buy From the Jews!"

The antisemitic platform of the Nazis, and particularly the announcement of this boycott, caused a strong reaction outside Germany. Newspapers in the UNITED STATES and GREAT BRITAIN criticized the boycott. On 27 March 1933, a massive protest rally was called by the American Jewish Congress in New York. It threatened a counter-boycott of all German goods until the anti-Jewish action was called off. Many Jewish and anti-Nazi groups imposed their own bans on German products (see BOYCOTTS, ANTI-NAZI). These international protests led the Nazis to

officially limit the boycott to one day. However, one week later, they imposed laws that restricted Jewish professionals and government officials.

BOYCOTT, ANTI-NAZI

A Jewish defense mechanism established in reaction to the Nazi persecution of German Jewry. On 19 March 1933, the Jewish War Veterans of America announced that its members would not buy German goods and services and it would discourage others from doing so. Similar boycott groups arose spontaneously in POLAND, among Jews in PALESTINE, (Israel) in FRANCE and elsewhere.

Despite widespread support among the average Jewish citizen, many Jewish organizations opposed the boycott. They feared that a Jewish boycott would play into the hands of Nazi propaganda, by seeming to prove the existence of a Jewish conspiracy against GERMANY. They feared brutal retaliation against German Jews.

The boycott met with only limited success, since

Boycott poster in the window of a Jewish-owned women's clothing store in Berlin. Next to the sign someone has drawn a road sign bearing the words "To Jerusalem"

it was not always pursued effectively. Yet, even if it had been more faithfully pursued, it is not clear that Jews really possessed the financial power to have any real effect on the German economy.

> Our people would be justified in seeing to it that nowhere in the world and under no circumstances should a Jew, from this day forth, buy or use merchandise manufactured in Germany or support German industry in any form.
>
> Statement by an American Jewish leader, Samuel Untermeyer, in The New York Times, 14 April 1933.

BRAND, JOEL JENÖ

(1906–1964) Member of the RELIEF AND RESCUE COMMITTEE OF BUDAPEST. In his early childhood his family moved from HUNGARY to GERMANY. In 1934, after the Nazis rose to power, he returned to Budapest. Brand and his wife Hansi, became involved in helping refugees from AUSTRIA, Germany, CZECHOSLOVAKIA and POLAND.

Following the Nazi invasion of Hungary in 1944, the Nazi agent Dieter WISLICENY contacted Brand. Wisliceny brought letters from Rabbi Michael Dov WEISSMANDEL and others in SLOVAKIA that said that by bribing Nazi agents they had been able to delay DEPORTATIONS. Wisliceny introduced Brand (and later Rudolph KASZTNER) to Adolf EICHMANN, who informed them of the price of ransoming the Jews remaining in Hungary and in neighboring countries. Brand was to convey this information to the Allies. The Nazis demanded hundreds of tons of soap, coffee, cocoa and tea in addition to 10,000 trucks which they guaranteed would only be used on the Eastern front.

Eichmann sent Brand to Istanbul, where he arrived on 19 May 1944. Brand immediately sought out the Zionist representatives there, presented his credentials and informed them that it was urgent that he inform Eichmann that the Allies might agree to the deal. If so, Eichmann might stop the deportations from Hungary that had started in early May. He might even let some Jews escape in order to show his good faith. The Zionists, satisfied about Brand's honesty, including his report that 12,000 Jews were being deported daily, reported the matter to the British authorities in the Middle East. Brand was also interviewed by American representatives in Turkey. His interviewer on behalf of the AMERICAN JOINT DISTRIBUTION COMMITTEE advised his office "to keep all avenues of negotiations open;" while the U.S. Vice-Consul reported that "this was part of an effort to split the Allies." The British government, after consulting with the Americans and the Russians and considering the matter for several weeks, turned down the deal. Brand was detained by the British in Aleppo (Syria), after the offer was rejected.

Brand asked to be allowed to return to Budapest. Instead he was taken to Cairo and interrogated at great length. The intelligence officer reported that Brand "seemed a very naive idealist." Nonetheless, he was not permitted to return to Europe during the war.

After the war Brand devoted his time to finding Nazi war criminals. He gave evidence in the EICHMANN TRIAL in Jerusalem, and died while giving evidence in the Frankfurt trial of two of Eichmann's assistants, Otto Hunsche and Hermann Krumey.

BRANDT, KARL

(?–1948) German physician and later general Reich commissioner for sanitation and health (with "special assignments"). Brandt received his medical license in 1928. He became a member of the NAZI PARTY in 1932. Brandt was appointed Adolf HITLER's personal physician in 1934. In 1939, Hitler signed an order empowering him to put to death those considered unsuitable to live. What followed was the EUTHANASIA PROGRAM, in which men, women and children who were physically disabled, mentally retarded or emotionally disturbed, were systematically killed. He was also involved in other ghastly MEDICAL EXPERIMENTS.

Following WORLD WAR II, he was brought to trial for his role in carrying out "cruel medical experiments with often fatal results" on concentration camp inmates and prisoners of war. He was convicted of crimes against humanity, sentenced to death by a United States military court and executed.

BRITISH UNION OF FASCISTS (BUF)

see MOSLEY, SIR OSWALD.

BRUNNER, ALOIS

(1912–) Nazi official who directed many deportations of Jews to death camps. He was born in AUSTRIA, joined the NAZI PARTY in 1931, and the SS in 1938. He was appointed director of the Office for Jewish Emigration, which was established by Adolf EICHMANN in VIENNA. In November 1939, he supervised the first deportation of Jews from that city. In November 1942, with his task in Vienna nearly done, he was called to BERLIN. On 12 January 1943, the first train of deportees left the German capital. The city was declared *Judenrein*, free of Jews, on 16 June of the same year. Meanwhile, in March 1943, Brunner had been sent to GREECE to carry out the deportation of Jews from SALONIKA, Thrace, and MACEDONIA with maximum speed. From there he went to the DRANCY concentration camp in FRANCE, following complaints that deportations were not going fast enough. In September 1943, he left Drancy for Nice. There he supervised the mass deportation of Jews who had found refuge in the previously non-occupied part of France. A year later (September 1944), he was in Bratislava to round up and deport the last Jews of SLOVAKIA. Brunner disappeared at the end of the war. He was sentenced to death—in his absence—in 1954 in France for crimes committed in that country. According to reports, he was still living in Damascus, Syria, in 1996.

BUCHAREST

Capital city of ROMANIA. In the late 1930s, about 100,000 JEWS lived there. Their situation grew worse and worse. They had been badly hit by antisemitic laws in the regime of Octavian GOGA since late 1937. Many lost their jobs when Jews were expelled from the Chamber of Commerce and most trade unions. Attacks on Jews and their property increased as antisemitic groups grew stronger. When Ion ANTONESCU came to power in 1940, his fascist (see FASCISM AND FASCIST MOVEMENTS) supporters from the IRON GUARD terrorized the Jews. When Antonescu tried to curb the Iron Guards, they openly rebelled. During the three day revolt in January 1941, Iron Guard members roamed the streets of Bucharest looking for Jews to attack and for Jewish-owned property to loot. One hundred Jews arrested on the first day were shot to death. Others were subjected to torture or humiliation. One hundred twenty-seven had died and hundreds were wounded by the time Antonescu put down the rebellion and restored order. There was tremendous damage to property, including synagogues.

Antonescu continued with his severe anti-Jewish measures, especially in Bucharest. Jews were fired from the jobs they still held and thrown out of their homes. CHILDREN were dismissed from schools. FORCED LABOR, compulsory for Jews aged 16 to 60. Jewish leaders and professionals were forced to sweep the streets and clear snow in winter. Antonescu ordered Jews from other parts of the country, who had come to Bucharest in search of greater

The ruins of a synagogue which was burned during the Bucharest pogrom of January 1941

security, to leave the city. In September 1942, several hundred Jews were deported to TRANSNISTRIA, where most were killed. Many buildings and homes belonging to Jews were taken from them. Outrageous taxes forced the community into poverty. Jewish institutions, assisted by the Federation of Jewish Communities, organized temporary housing and schools, and distributed much needed supplies. Community leaders, such as Wilhelm Filderman and Chief Rabbi Alexander Safran, succeeded in stopping some measures, such as wearing the Jewish BADGE or placing Jews in GHETTOS.

In August 1944, as the Soviet army approached, King Michael had Antonescu arrested. Although they had been through severe suffering, the Jews of Bucharest were saved from DEPORTATIONS and mass killing.

B U C H E N W A L D

Concentration camp in GERMANY. The camp was opened in July 1937 and was known for its terrible conditions even before the outbreak of WORLD WAR II. The first people sent to Buchenwald were political prisoners and criminals. Beginning in June 1938 large groups of Jews were sent there. In November 1938, after KRISTALLNACHT, an additional 10,000 Jews from Germany and AUSTRIA were imprisoned in the camp. They were forced to work in its quarry under brutal conditions. The real purpose of this cruelty was to force the Jews and their families to flee Germany, and eventually many of these inmates were released.

In October 1942, an order was given for all Jewish prisoners held by Germany to be moved to AUSCHWITZ. Thus, the number of Jewish prisoners at Buchenwald fell until May 1944, when large transports of Hungarian Jews arrived from Auschwitz. The number of prisoners climbed to over 89,000. Jews were not allowed the privileges that other prisoners received, and some were used for MEDICAL EXPERIMENTS. The harsh and unhygienic conditions led to deaths in great numbers. Over 600 CHILDREN were housed in "Children's Block 66."

In Buchenwald, an underground was formed and succeeded in carrying out many acts of sabotage. Some took place in the armaments factory where inmates worked. Underground members working in

Survivor drinking from a metal bowl in front of a barracks in Buchenwald after liberation, 1945

Buchenwald's offices succeeded in changing final ss orders to evacuate Buchenwald completely. As a result, the Nazis failed to achieve their aim of sending most inmates to their deaths before the war's end. By the time the American forces arrived to liberate the camp, armed prisoners were in control. At liberation, 21,000 prisoners were freed. Four thousand were Jews, including 1,000 children and young people.

In 1947, 31 members of the Buchenwald staff were put on trial for war crimes. Two were sentenced to death and four to life imprisonment. Of the nearly 240,000 prisoners held at the camp from the time it opened, 43,045 died or were murdered there.

The site of the concentration camp can be visited today and some of the original buildings, including the crematorium, have been preserved.

B U D A P E S T

Capital of HUNGARY. Jewish settlement in Budapest can be traced back to Roman times. In 1941, there were 184,473 Jews and some 62,000 persons of Jewish origin affected by the anti-Jewish legislation in Budapest out of a total population of 1.7 million. Jews played an important role in the city's life: in the professions, finance, commerce, industry, journalism, literature, theater, music, arts and sports.

While antisemitism was always present in Hungary, "solving the Jewish Question" became government policy only after Hungary joined the Axis in 1935. Starting with the First Jewish Law in 1938, anti-Jewish legislation reduced the number of Jewish wage earners to 5 percent of all employees. The exclusion of Jews from professional associations prevented them from practicing. As a result of these and other factors, the community's resources were drastically reduced. In 1941, further legislation deprived Jewish communities of their right to levy taxes. This, and the additional burden of equipping Jews called for FORCED LABOR, further weakened the community. Between 1941 and March 1944, 21,386 Jewish men from Budapest lost their lives in labor camps on the eastern front. However, comparatively speaking, the Jews of Budapest were less affected by persecutions until 1944.

The Nazi invasion of Budapest in March 1944

Suvivors and American soldiers in the central courtyard in Buchenwald after liberation, 1945

On 16 October 1944, the massacre of Budapest Jews began.... We heard a tremendous noise like dynamite going off and that was it. Twenty-two SS men came in with machine guns, guns and hand grenades. They threw the hand grenades into the doors and they said, "All the Jews downstairs. Put your coats on and go downstairs." So, we put our coats on and they lined us up in the street. The street lights were darkened because of the air raids. They lined us up 8 abreast and they surrounded us on both sides. They drew their machine guns and told the neighboring occupants of the building to go inside.... Then the SS man started shooting. But Mother had padded me the day before and this day too when we went to the air raid shelter. I always had sardine cans and chocolate because Mother said, "If anything happens...you have to have some food...and we won't starve if they are taking us.... I was such a skinny girl that when she padded me nothing showed, and I had all those sardine cans and canned food and three pullovers...and I had my coat on. So, he continued shooting and all those machine gun bullets came down...and tore apart my coat, tore apart the cans of sardines but didn't hit my heart.... They were diverted by the cans of food and the chocolates....

From the testimony of Eva Wahrman Bentley, Gratz College Holocaust Oral History Archive

introduced the familiar pattern of persecution, with the willing participation of the non-Jewish population and the police. After appointing a Jewish Council, JUDENRAT, the GESTAPO immediately arrested several hundred prominent Jews as hostages. The beds of the main Jewish hospital were taken for the SS; all Jewish-owned stores were closed; 1,500 apartments were turned over for the use of non-Jews. In June, the Jews of Budapest were ordered to crowd into 2,639 designated buildings. Many were arrested. By this time, the rest of the Hungarian Jewry had been deported to their deaths in AUSCHWITZ. In July 1944,

Jewish women being led through the streets of Budapest to concentration camps, 1944

the deportations were temporarily suspended, but many Jews searched for hiding places should they be renewed. They were aided by the Swedish diplomat Raoul WALLENBERG, the Swiss diplomat Carl LUTZ and others who got false papers and safe houses for them. These actions saved tens of thousands of Jews.

In August, Miklós HORTHY sought contact with the Allies, declaring Hungary's withdrawal from the war on 15 October 1944. Within 24 hours, he was arrested by the Germans and a new government under the ARROW CROSS (the Hungarian Fascist party) leader Ferenc SZÁLASI took over. They began a reign of terror. Adolf EICHMANN came to Budapest and 70,000 Jews were moved into the GHETTO.

From 8 November to 24 December 1944, 76,000 Jews were marched to the Austrian border. Thousands of men were forced to dig trenches around the city. As many as 20,000 were shot and thrown into the Danube river; hundreds died in the ghetto from starvation and disease. The liquidation of the ghetto was scheduled for mid-January, but the Red Army liberated the city on 18 January 1945. At this time only 120,000 Jews remained alive. They included those in the ghetto and in houses protected by neutral powers, those emerging from hiding using the forged documents supplied by the Zionist underground, and a few—chiefly converts—hidden by the churches.

B U K O V I N A

Territory in east-central Europe, divided between ROMANIA and the UKRAINE. Bukovina came under Austrian rule in 1775. After World War I, it became part of Romania. Much of the Jewish population was German-speaking and identified with Austrian culture. On the eve of the Holocaust, there were about 100,000 Jews in the area.

Northern Bukovina, including the city of Czernowitz (today Cernauti or Chernovtsy), was annexed by SOVIET RUSSIA in 1940. Romanian soldiers had murdered hundreds of Jews even before the annexation. Under the Russians, Jewish institutions were shut down and many leading Jews were arrested and deported to Soviet LABOR CAMPS. The region was re-taken by Romanian and German troops in July 1941, and the Nazis began to murder imme-

diately. In some of the smaller towns, thousands of Jews were killed by local mobs even before the German and Romanian soldiers arrived.

After the Nazis arrived, Jews were forced to wear the yellow BADGE. In October, a GHETTO was established in Czernowitz. Some 30,000 Jews from that city and 35,000 more from the countryside were deported from there to TRANSNISTRIA and were subjected to FORCED LABOR. The DEPORTATIONS were halted in November 1941, but began again in the summer of 1942. About half the Jewish population died. The territory was liberated by the Soviet army in Spring 1944. After the war, most of the survivors fled to Romania and from there to ISRAEL.

B U L G A R I A

Country in eastern Europe. The Jews of Bulgaria and DENMARK were the only two communities under Nazi rule that were saved from destruction. About 50,000 Jews were living in Bulgaria in the 1930s.

Metropolitan Cyril (right-after the war). One of the saviors of Bulgarian Jews

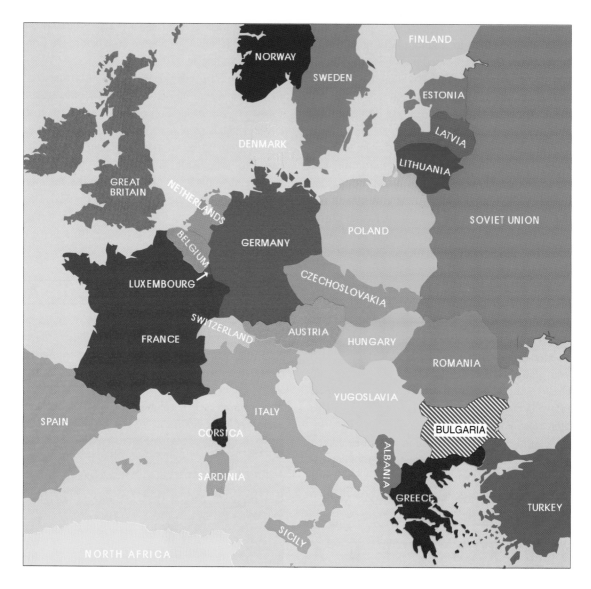

More than half were in the capital, Sofia, where they were 9 percent of the population. Bulgaria's history was remarkably free of antisemitism. In the 1930s, anti-Jewish viewpoints began to be expressed in certain political circles. Bulgaria joined the German-Italian Axis in March 1941 in the hope of receiving back territory taken from it after World War I. Bulgaria declared war on the Western Allies, and regained the provinces of Thrace (today in GREECE) and MACEDONIA in return. Units of the German army were stationed in Bulgaria, whose government was not completely taken over by the Nazis.

A pro-German government passed the first anti-Jewish laws in late 1940. These laws sparked protests in many segments of Bulgaria's population,

but they were still passed by the Bulgarian parliament. This led to an increase in strong measures against the Jews. They were dismissed from teaching posts, forced to wear the yellow BADGE, and to live in overcrowded conditions. Jews were barred from main streets and places of entertainment. Radios, cars and other valuables and were confiscated. Most Jewish men were drafted into FORCED LABOR. In September 1942, a Commissariat for Jewish Affairs was established, headed by Alexander Belev, a leading antisemite. The Commissariat, funded from blocked Jewish bank accounts, became the supreme body responsible for Jewish affairs.

In the winter of 1943, the German SS officer Theodor Dannecker was sent to Bulgaria to direct the policy against the Jews. At that time, the danger of the deportation of Bulgarian Jewry to death camps became a real possibility. In February 1943 the Bulgarian Interior Ministry agreed to deport Jews from the Bulgarian-occupied provinces of Macedonia and Thrace. The quota for deportees was 20,000, but since fewer than that number were living in those provinces, the difference of some 6,000 was to be made up by Jews from Bulgaria proper. As a first step 11,384 Jews were deported from Thrace and Macedonia to death in TREBLINKA.

The first group of Bulgarian Jews slated for deportation was from the town of Kyustendil, where Jews had lived for centuries in friendly relations with their non-Jewish neighbors. Dimiter Peshev, a vice-president of the local parliament, immediately opened a campaign supported by the citizens of the town to prevent the action. He met with the minister of interior and demanded that the deportation order be cancelled. The minister agreed—but only for the Jews of Bulgaria, not for those of Thrace and Macedonia. Peshev then organized a petition of protest which he took to the prime minister, demanding that all persecution of the Jews be stopped. The prime minister's reaction was to dismiss Peshev from the vice-presidency. The Germans continued their demand for the deportation of Bulgarian Jews. The government decided to expel the Jews of Sofia to the provinces (25–27 May 1943) and may have intended this as a first step toward their deportation. Thus, 20,000 Jews were sent to 20 provincial centers inside Bulgaria. While this was the most severe action taken against the Jews, it meant that the threat of deportation had passed. However, all male Jews between the ages of 20 and 46 were drafted into special labor battalions, to perform backbreaking tasks in the mountains and forests.

However, as the tide of war turned against the Germans, conditions gradually improved. The deported Jews of Sofia were allowed short visits home and other concessions. In August 1944, on the eve of the entry of the Russian Red Army, into Bulgaria, all anti-Jewish measures were abolished. The Jews of Bulgaria were persecuted—but they had been saved. In 1948–1949, 90 percent of Bulgarian Jews moved to ISRAEL, largely motivated by their Holocaust experience.

B U N A

see AUSCHWITZ.

B Y E L O R U S S I A

(Also Belorussia, Belarus, White Russia) Area situated between RUSSIA and POLAND, bordered by Latvia and LITHUANIA to the north and UKRAINE to the south. After centuries of Russian and/or Polish rule, Byelorussia became independent in 1991 and was renamed Belarus. It became a member of the Commonwealth of Independent States (CIS).

At the turn of the century there was a vibrant, well-organized Jewish community in Byelorussia, and Jews made up more than half the population of many towns and villages. After World War I, it was split between Soviet Russia (which ruled Eastern Byelorussia) and Poland. Following the German invasion of Poland in September 1939, the Soviet Union also occupied Western Byelorussia under the terms of the NAZI-SOVIET PACT concluded a few weeks earlier. A number of Jews from western Poland managed to escape to the area now occupied by the Soviet Union. By the time Germany invaded the Soviet Union on 22 June 1941, there were nearly 700,000 Jews in Western Byelorussia. Following the invasion, local populations launched a series of spontaneous attacks on Jews. The Germans gave them a free hand and then took over with a number of murderous "AKTIONS," in which nearly half the Jews of the area were killed and buried in mass graves. That first phase was followed by full-scale implementation of the "FINAL SOLUTION," in which almost all the Jews of Byelorussia were killed. Youth and Zionist movements tried to put up a fight and set up some form of RESISTANCE or underground movement almost everywhere.

With no help from local populations, and sometimes active opposition from them, their fight was doomed. Some 25,000 Jews did manage to escape into the forests and organize into guerrilla groups. Of the 400,000 Jews who lived in Eastern Byelorussia before the German invasion, 120,000 managed to flee inside Russia. The rest were killed, 100,000 of them in the ghetto of Minsk, which was liquidated in October 1943.

C A M P S

Three types of camps stand out from the Nazi period: CONCENTRATION CAMPS, LABOR CAMPS and DEATH CAMPS. Additional types of camps included detention camps, transit camps, camps of assembly and prisoner-of-war camps. Altogether the Nazis established 3,000 camps throughout Europe.

Concentration camps were first established in 1933, immediately after Adolf HITLER's rise to power. The first inmates of these camps were Jews, communists and other opponents of the Nazi regime. Also imprisoned were political opponents of the THIRD REICH, social outcasts, and the physically and mentally handicapped. The stated objective of these camps was to "reform" political opponents

Major concentration, forced labor, transit and extermination camps in Europe, World War II

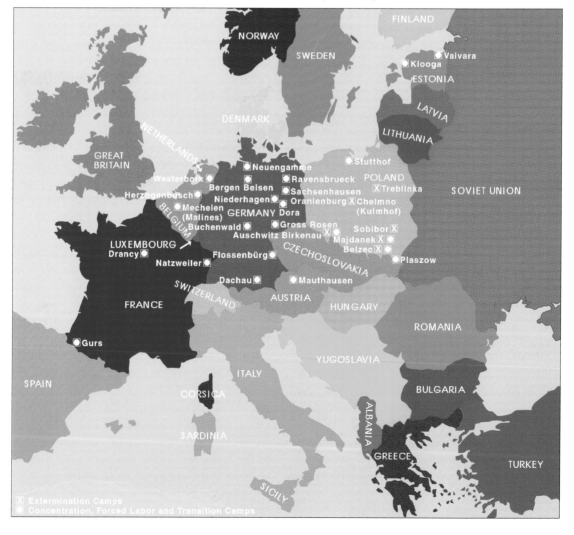

and "to change the anti-social members of society into useful citizens." The inmates were never brought before a judge or to trial, and were never permitted to appeal for justice. Between 1933 and 1939, over 200,000 people were detained in concentration camps.

Labor camps were generally smaller and connected to an industrial area whose administrative headquarters were in a nearby larger camp. It was common practice for many of the inmates to live in other facilities and to be marched off to these works sites. Many were worked to death.

With the 1941 decision to kill all Jews, a number of camps in POLAND were transformed into DEATH CAMPS. They became the means through

Left: Interior of a barrack in Auschwitz-Birkenau; Below: Aerial view of the Birkenau death complex

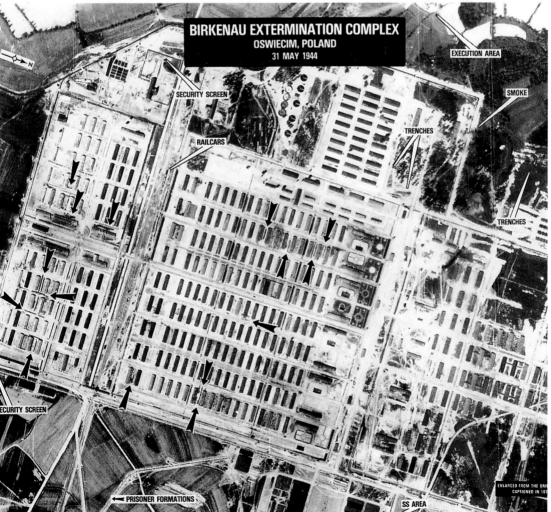

BIRKENAU EXTERMINATION COMPLEX
OSWIECIM, POLAND
31 MAY 1944

EXECUTION AREA

SECURITY SCREEN

SMOKE

TRENCHES

RAILCARS

TRENCHES

SECURITY SCREEN

PRISONER FORMATIONS

SS AREA

ENLARGED FROM THE ORIG
CAPTIONED IN 197

which the Nazis could carry out their plan to murder the Jews of Europe. Although killing Jews was their primary purpose, others who died in these camps included HOMOSEXUALS, GYPSIES and SOVIET PRISONERS OF WAR.

C A N A D A

British Commonwealth country in North America that entered the war against GERMANY shortly after the German invasion of POLAND. Canada played a significant role in bringing about the Allied victory. However, Canada's efforts to help ease the plight of the Nazi's Jewish victims stands out as disproportionately small given its immense land mass. Canada simply refused to grant sanctuary to Jewish refugees from the Nazi slaughter.

Canada's restrictive immigration policies for Jews predated the Nazi era. From 1923 on the Canadian government limited Jewish immigration to those who had close relatives already living in Canada. As a result, during the decade that saw the Nazis overrun Europe (1931–1941) fewer than 1,500 Jews were permitted to enter Canada. Documentary evi-

Canadian liberators examining the crematorium at the concentration camp in Vught, The Netherlands

> *"Canada" was also the name given to the warehouse at Auschwitz where the valuables taken from incoming prisoners were stored. In these huge storerooms everything from blankets and pots to jewelry and human hair was sorted and sent back to Germany.*

dence indicates that Canada was a reluctant participant in both the EVIAN CONFERENCE on the problem of refugees and the BERMUDA CONFERENCE. Apparently, its main concern was that it not be proposed as a location for resettling refugees. Even its single humanitarian gesture to accept 1,000 Jewish children from VICHY France whose parents had been deported to Poland, came too late. By the time the rescue plan was approved, these children had already been sent to join their parents in the DEATH CAMPS. Thus, Jewish immigration to Canada during the entire Holocaust period was not significant.

Canada's policy toward Jewish immigration has been summarized in the words of the anonymous Canadian official who said, "None is too many," when commenting about how many Jews should be allowed into Canada. While too late for the millions who had lost their lives, Canada did change its immigration policies in 1948 when restrictions against Jewish immigration were removed.

CANARIS, WILHELM

(1887–1945) German admiral, chief of the ABWEHR—the German military intelligence—(1935–1944) and main organizer of German aid to General Franco during the Spanish Civil War.

Canaris was a World War I hero, who was taken prisoner and escaped to rejoin his unit. He was eager to avenge his country's defeat. At first he supported the Nazi movement, since he was convinced that SOVIET RUSSIA and communism were a major threat to GERMANY. He was soon disappointed, when he realized that Nazism was a threat to German heritage and tradition. After the German invasion of POLAND, he protested the atrocities committed against aristocratic and church leaders. His sympathy grew for HITLER's opponents within the military,

Wilhelm Canaris

since he believed that the war would ultimately destroy Germany. This led him to admit some of these opponents into the ranks of military intelligence in order to give them protection. The SS became suspicious of his activities after the assassination of Reinhard HEYDRICH in 1942. However, because of the high quality of German intelligence and the spectacular operations realized under his direction, the SS did not dare touch him. It was only after some of his best agents had defected to the West, toward the end of the war, that the SS succeeded in having Canaris demoted and transferred to the economic section of the army in February 1944. Kept under close watch, he was eventually arrested after the attempt on Adolf Hitler's life on 20 July 1944. He was executed by the GESTAPO on charges of treason on 9 April 1945, following a direct order by Hitler.

CENTRE DE DOCUMENTATION JUIVE CONTEMPORAINE

("Center of Contemporary Jewish Documentation") Central archives of the French Jewish community relating to the Holocaust, established in 1943.

Isaac Schneerson was a Russian Jew who had become a French industrialist. In 1943, he was a refugee from the Nazis in southern FRANCE. He felt it was important both to preserve the archives of the Jewish communities of France and to document their destruction. He established the center as part of the UNDERGROUND movement in the unoccupied zone of France. After the war, it was moved to PARIS.

Today, it is one of the leading Holocaust archives in the world. It contains transcripts of all the major TRIALS OF WAR CRIMINALS that were conducted in France, as well as complete records of all DEPORTATIONS from France during the war. It is also the site of a memorial to the unknown Jewish martyr.

CHELMNO (Kulmhof)

The first of the DEATH CAMPS to use gassing, and the first place outside Soviet territory in which Jews were systematically killed as part of the "FINAL SOLUTION."

The camp was situated 47 miles west of LÓDZ in POLAND and was to serve as the killing center for the Jews of Lódz. Unlike other death camps, railroad lines did not reach directly into Chelmno. Jews were sent by freight train to the nearest railroad station, and from there they were transferred to Chelmno by truck.

Like AUSCHWITZ, Chelmno consisted of two sites. The camp in Schloss, which was an old manorhouse, was where prisoners were processed and killed and where the camp staff lived. Two and a half miles away, near a forest, was a second camp called Waldlanger. It was the site of mass graves and later of the crematoria ovens.

The first victims arrived at Chelmno on 7 December 1941, and gassing began the very next day. Arriving prisoners were brought by truck to the reception area, where their possessions were confiscated and they were forced to undress. They were then sent to the cellar, to a room designated as the "washroom." Then they were forced down a ramp into awaiting gas vans.

These vans were converted Renault trucks, which looked like furniture trucks. Fifty to seventy prisoners were forced in at one time. The engine was started and the exhaust was piped into the sealed compartment. Death came within 10 minutes.

The dead were then transported by these trucks to the Waldlanger camp, where they were unloaded and buried in mass graves. Crematoria were later built on the site to cremate the bodies. In the last months of the war, the bodies of those who had been killed earlier were dug up and burned (see AKTION 1005).

Some 320,000 Jews were killed at Chelmno, primarily from Lódz and the surrounding WARTHEGAU region. Also killed were several hundred Poles, some 5,000 GYPSIES from Lódz, and 88 Czech children from LIDICE.

The killing at Chelmno was suspended in March 1943, when nearly all the Jewish populations of the region had been murdered. It began again for a time in June 1944, when the Lódz ghetto was liquidated. The camp was abandoned by the Germans on 17 January 1945.

In the TRIALS OF WAR CRIMINALS that followed the war, the Chelmno staff received few major sentences. Three officials were sentenced to 13 years in prison, one to 7 years and the others received light punishment.

A monument was built in Chelmno after the war. The Poles have built a new monument on the site of the crematoria incorporating pieces of the crematoria, and a small display explains what happened at Chelmno.

C H E T N I K S

A name for guerrilla movements in SERBIA, which comes from the Serbian word for "platoon." During WORLD WAR II it referred to Serbian fighters in YUGOSLAVIA. After the German occupation of the country, a number of former soldiers, including Jews, took refuge in the mountains of central Serbia.

Jewish prisoners digging their own grave in Chelmno death camp

In April 1941, there they were organized into guerrilla units by Colonel Draza Mihajlovic, a former officer of the Yugoslav army. Their aim was to restore the royal house of Serbia, and they were therefore bitterly opposed to the resistance leader Josip Broz Tito and his communist partisans. Nevertheless, in the summer of 1941, the Chetniks reluctantly allied themselves with Tito to fight the common enemy, GERMANY. They failed and suffered heavy casualties.

Mihajlovic became convinced that his forces would never be able to defeat the Germans. He then decided that his first duty was to make sure that Yugoslavia would not become communist after the war. To that end, he had to fight Tito and his partisans. After several months of fierce infighting, the Chetniks began to cooperate with the German and Italian forces against Tito. Jews began leaving the Chetnik camp. By the end of 1943, the Chetniks were solidly entrenched in the Nazi camp. This led them to commit a number of attacks against Jews and Jewish property. In some cases, they even handed Jews over to the Germans.

When the Soviet army took over Serbia with the help of Tito and his partisans, they hunted down the Chetniks. Mihajlovic was captured as were most of his men. A national tribunal set up at the end of the war found them guilty of treason. They were condemned to death and hanged.

C H I L D R E N

One and a half million Jewish children are estimated to have been murdered during the Holocaust. Only 11 percent of the Jewish children who were alive in Europe at the start of WORLD WAR II survived to its end. Historians face problems in documenting the experiences of these children. They often were not included in Nazi records, and few survived to tell their own stories. A small number of children did keep diaries during the Holocaust, and adults also wrote about the children around them. The experience of each child was unique.

In GERMANY (and later in AUSTRIA and CZECHOSLOVAKIA) in the 1930s, children were affected by ANTI-JEWISH LEGISLATION. They were barred from German schools and youth groups. Many suffered antisemitic taunts and attacks from other children who had previously been their friends. Many children witnessed their parents being arrested and taken to CONCENTRATION CAMPS. Some parents chose to send their children away from Germany in the late 1930s. Ten thousand unaccompanied children reached GREAT BRITAIN on the KINDERTRANSPORTS in the years before the war broke out. They had to adjust to a new culture and learn a new language without the support of their parents. The majority lived with foster parents and never saw their real parents again.

During the war, many children were herded into GHETTOS in POLAND and Russia with their parents. They were not entitled to food rations of their own. Orphaned children were forced to beg or steal food. Conditions were so bad that most children in the ghettos died of malnutrition and disease. Some young people escaped the ghettos and joined PARTISANS and RESISTANCE groups fighting against the Nazis.

Thousands of Jewish children were shot alongside their families by the EINSATZGRUPPEN during the invasion of SOVIET RUSSIA in 1941. After 1942, Jewish (and GYPSY) children from all over Europe were sent to the Polish DEATH CAMPS at TREBLINKA, SOBIBÓR and

Homeless children in the Warsaw Ghetto

BELZEC. Children were immediately sent to the GAS CHAMBERS with very few exceptions. In AUSCHWITZ and MAJDANEK there were selections. Older children who looked as though they could work were spared the gas chamber. The few children who were selected to live, were robbed of their youth when they entered the camps. In order to survive they had to behave like adults, and they endured the same horrible conditions as the adults. Children were not spared the cruel MEDICAL EXPERIMENTS conducted by Nazi doctors. For example, Josef MENGELE selected young twins from the transports to use in his tests.

Thousands of Jewish children spent part of the war in hiding. Anne FRANK is a famous example. She hid from the Nazis with her family in a warehouse attic in Amsterdam, but in the end was betrayed and sent to her death. Most children in hiding were not lucky enough to have their families by their sides. UNDERGROUND rescue operations were mounted in many countries, including FRANCE and Poland, in order to conceal children or to get them over an international border to safety. Many were sent to convents or orphanages or fostered by strangers. Often

they had to pretend to be Christian and take on a new name and religion. Life in hiding was usually very frightening. Children were always in danger of being discovered.

In the concentration camps and ghettos it was usually illegal to educate children or involve them in any cultural activity. Adults risked their lives to teach children basic lessons in cramped and filthy conditions. They tried to bring some normality to the children's lives by talking to them about literature and art. Children's homes were established in the ghettos. The most famous was run by Janusz KORCZAK in the WARSAW ghetto. He cared for and educated over 100 orphans at any one time. In some transit camps, like WESTERBORK, families were allowed to live together. Organized lessons were planned with the limited books available. Formal education was forbidden in THERESIENSTADT, but an active underground program was organized there too. In 1942, children formed 10 percent of the population in that camp. The Jewish Council (JUDENRAT) there established a Youth Welfare department. Young people were educated secretly, in particular about

Children in the Warsaw Ghetto, 1942

freedom and democracy. The art work and poetry created by Jewish children in this camp have survived, but are an exception.

CHILDREN'S DIARIES

see DIARIES, HOLOCAUST.

CHRISTIAN CHURCHES AND THE HOLOCAUST

In 1933, most Catholics and Protestants in GERMANY welcomed the rise of Nazism. They believed Adolf HITLER's claim that Nazism would support "positive Christianity." However, the Nazis soon began interfering in Christian affairs, and trying to do away with religious education. Christian leaders then began to be more critical of the government.

Christians did not want the Nazis to interfere in the churches since they believed that religious faith should be independent of Nazi ideology. Catholic and Protestant leaders were concerned about Nazism's growing powerful hold on all parts of German society. These leaders hoped to prevent government control of their churches, even though they agreed with many of the Nazis' political aims. Only the small groups of non-conformist "Free Churches"—notably the QUAKERS and Jehovah's Witnesses—openly opposed Nazism from the beginning.

The Catholic and Protestant churches tried to make some arrangements with the Nazis, since they hoped that compromise would protect their churches, schools and their priests and nuns. In July 1933, representatives of the the Vatican and the Nazi regime signed a concordat in which the Church recognized the legitimacy of the Nazi state. The Nazis, in turn, promised not to interfere with Catholic organizations and religious schools. One reason for Christian (especially Vatican) failure to condemn Nazism was the belief that Nazism was holding back Russian communism. They saw communism as the greater danger to religion.

During the same period, the Protestant Church came under strong government pressure. This led to serious divisions within the Church between Nazi supporters (the "German Christians"), opponents, and moderates. Moderate leaders were determined to prevent unrest in the Protestant Church. They

therefore made many compromises with the Nazis. In contrast, about one-third of German Protestant pastors joined the Confessing Church, an anti-Nazi grouping of Evangelical churches. Some Confessing Christians—notably Dietrich BONHOEFFER and Martin NIEMÖLLER—were eventually imprisoned for their opposition to the Nazi regime. Others actively worked to help JEWS hide or escape Germany (see "RIGHTEOUS AMONG THE NATIONS").

For the most part, however, Catholic and Protestant Churches were more concerned with protecting themselves than with helping the Jews. The long tradition of Christian ANTISEMITISM partly explained this. Even in the Confessing Church, it was mostly those who had converted from Judaism to Christianity who supported the Jews. Most Church leaders were silent and did not protest against Nazi persecution of Jews, even after the KRISTALLNACHT pogrom in November 1938.

Outside Germany, the situation was more mixed. The Vatican's attitude toward the Nazis was to be carefully neutral. This included the refusal of Pope PIUS XII to publicly condemn the DEPORTATIONS of Jews—even from Rome. However, Italian Catholics helped to save many of the country's Jews. Elsewhere, there was more protest against Nazi policies. The Dutch Catholic Church forbade its members to join the Dutch NAZI PARTY in 1934, and later openly protested the deportations of Dutch Jews. Nazi measures against the Jews drew strong protests from the Lutheran Churches of NORWAY, SWEDEN, and DENMARK.

In general, however, the international Christian community was slow to respond to what was happening to the Jews. There were a few leaders who tried to awaken the world to the seriousness of the Nazi measures. After Kristallnacht, Christian leaders in Geneva sent a letter to churches throughout the world warning, "At the moment when the terrible persecution of the Jewish population in Germany and in other central European countries has come to a violent climax, it is our duty to remind ourselves of the stand which we have taken as a movement of all Christian churches against antisemitism in all its forms."

In 1942, after the mass murders became known, the Federal Council of Churches in the United States announced, "It is impossible to avoid the conclusion that something like a policy of deliberate extermination of the Jews in Europe is being carried out. The violence and inhumanity which Nazi leaders have publicly [taken] towards all Jews are apparently now coming to a climax in a virtual massacre. We are resolved to do our full part in establishing conditions in which such treatment of the Jews shall end." That same month, the newly formed British Council of Christians and Jews began a public campaign that called for the Allies to aid countries offering refuge to Jews.

For the most part, however, these appeals fell on deaf ears. The few Christian leaders who publicly protested against the murder of Europe's Jews received little support from the members of their churches. As a result, Christian churches inside and outside Germany are still wrestling with their guilt about the Holocaust. In the years since 1945, churches throughout the world have issued statements admitting their failure to halt the murder of the European Jews and condemning antisemitism. These statements have led to new thinking and understanding about Christianity's relationship with Judaism.

C H U R C H E S

see CHRISTIAN CHURCHES.

CHURCHILL, WINSTON LEONARD SPENCER

(1874–1965) Prime minister of GREAT BRITAIN from May 1940 until the end of WORLD WAR II in Europe. Churchill was one of the first British politicians to realize the dangers of Nazism. Throughout the 1930s, his was a lonely voice in the ruling Conservative Party in Britain, attacking Premier Neville Chamberlain's policy of APPEASEMENT of Adolf HITLER. With the failure of appeasement and the outbreak of war in September 1939, Churchill was invited to join the government as First Lord of the Admiralty (in charge of the British navy), a position he had held in World War I. After the fall of FRANCE in May 1940, the British parliament rejected Chamberlain and turned to Churchill to lead the country. Churchill was determined not to give in, but to fight the Germans to victory at all costs.

Churchill was fully aware of the terrible situation of the Jews of Europe. On a personal level, he was extremely sympathetic. However, he was convinced that forcing the Germans to surrender unconditionally was the most important goal. Helping the Jews could only come after that goal was achieved. Churchill was also a strong supporter of Zionism. He was in contact with the Zionist leader Chaim WEIZMANN, and favored the creation of a Jewish State with British support. He viewed this as a move that would also be in Great Britain's best interest.

Nevertheless, Churchill did not introduce any policies designed to help the Jews. He explained his reasoning for this in February 1943. He said that helping Jews escape from Nazi-occupied Europe would cause a transportation problem, as escape routes would have to pass through important military areas. He urged the Zionists to be patient and said that he hoped they would achieve their goal of establishing a Jewish State once the war had been won. However, after the war, he was no longer prime minister and a Labor government was in power.

COLLABORATORS

Members of the local population in a Nazi-occupied territory who helped the Germans oppress and murder the JEWS.

The responsibility for the deliberate isolation, plunder and murder of the Jews of Europe rests on the Germans. However, because of the very large area of the conquered territories, the Nazis could not have succeeded without the help of the local population. Local politicians, police, soldiers, and ordinary individuals throughout occupied Europe eagerly helped the Nazis. This included the murder of Jews. In many places in eastern Europe POGROMS were even started by local anti-Jewish groups. In both east and west, collaborators turned in Jews who were hiding to the authorities.

In FRANCE, for example, the Legion des Volontaires Français Contre le Bolchevism (Legion of French Volunteers Against Bolshevism) became a unit in the German army. It participated in the killing of Polish Jews in Radom in December 1942. In France itself the Parti Populaire Français, supporters of the VICHY government, participated directly in the

High ranking officers of the Ustasha (Croatian Militia)

rounding up of Jews for DEPORTATION. In ITALY, after the surrender to the Allies in 1943, the FASCIST Black Brigades assisted in rounding up Jews in the areas of Italy still occupiedby the Nazis. The ARROW CROSS in HUNGARY, participated in the slaughter of thousands of Jews. In SLOVAKIA, the HLINKA GUARDS helped with the deportations, as did the regular Slovak police. In ROMANIA, Jews were massacred both by the IRON GUARD and army units.

In the Polish and Soviet territories, the Germans had appointed local governments which were responsible directly to them. Here, there was widespread collaboration. Local leaders participated in forcing Jews into GHETTOS, deportations and murder. In VILNA, LITHUANIA, local officials forced the Jews into the ghetto and supervised the collection and storage of stolen Jewish property. In WARSAW, Polish police tracked down Jews escaping from the ghetto. In the Soviet territories, the Germans organized *Schutzmannschaft*. These were groups of local people to assist the Germans in their actions against the Jews, including murder. The *Schutzmannschaft* included Ukrainians, Byelorussians, Estonians, Lithuanians, Latvians and Russian cossacks. In the UKRAINE, local militia helped in slaughtering the Jews of Zhitomir, Korosten, Kherson, Radomyshl and

Kakhovka. In BYELORUSSIA, local police helped to liquidate the ghettos. In Estonia, the police were particularly brutal. For example, in September 1942, they slaughtered transports of Jews on their way to THERESIENSTADT. Estonians formed part of the guard at the Vaivara concentration camp, and murdered thousands there as well. Throughout Lithuania, local police and volunteers aided in assembling Jews and in the actual mass shootings. In LATVIA, locals engaged in mass shootings, particularly in the RIGA district. In short, both as part of the *Schutsmannschaft,* and as volunteers in specific actions, the local population played a major role in the murder of their Jewish neighbors.

COMMISSAR DECREE

SEE KOMMISSARBEFEHL.

CONCENTRATION CAMPS

CAMPS where opponents of the Nazis were imprisoned without trial. In the early years of Nazi rule, their purpose was to remove any actual or possible opposition to the NAZI PARTY. As the Nazis grew stronger in the 1930s, the concentration camps took on different roles. Even so, concentration camps should not be confused with DEATH CAMPS (although two of these, MAJDANEK and AUSCHWITZ, had concentration camps on their sites). Historians tend to divide the development of the concentration camps into three stages: 1933–1936; 1936–1942; and 1942–1945.

First phase, 1933–1936. Between February and July 1933, the Nazis attacked their political opponents in various ways. Communists, socialists, and trade unionists were taken into "protective custody" by the ss and local police authorities. Special camps were set up to house them, since the arrests were made outside the legal and court system. The first concentration camp was set up at DACHAU in March 1933. It served as the model for other camps established by the SS. These camps used brutal methods of control and "re-education," including hard labor, beatings, torture, and executions. In this first period, the majority of prisoners were released within a year.

At first no single organization controlled these camps. By spring 1934, however, they all came under the control of the SS, headed by Heinrich HIMMLER.

Second phase, 1936–1942. In 1936, Himmler was made chief of police. He authorized the imprisonment of what the Nazis termed "asocial" individuals: beggars, criminals, GYPSIES, and HOMOSEXUALS. All were considered a threat to the "purity" of German society. In 1938, for the first time, JEWS began to be sent to the camps in large numbers. They suffered a great deal but many were released when they promised that they would leave GERMANY.

After 1936, Germany began to prepare for war. Economics rather than politics began to play a part in the nature of the concentration camps. New camps were established at SACHSENHAUSEN (1936), BUCHENWALD (1937), MAUTHAUSEN (in AUSTRIA—1938), and RAVENSBRÜCK (1939). All of the original camps, except Dachau, were closed. The new camps were located near brick works or quarries. The SS set up factories nearby, where prisoners were forced to work. After the outbreak of war, independent concentration camps were also established in the occupied territories: Auschwitz (1940), Neuengamme (1940), NATZWEILER and GROSS-ROSEN (1941), and STUTTHOF (1942). Persons from other countries were bought to these camps, especially Polish political

prisoners, Jews, and SOVIET PRISONERS OF WAR.

During this second period, the concentration camps became centers of mass killing. Prisoners died through overwork and starvation. The daily routine was very harsh and conditions were overcrowded and subhuman. Typically, prisoners were forced out of their bunks early in the morning, made to stand in all weather for roll calls dressed in thin prison uniforms, and then forced to work for long hours. Food was poor and beatings common. The whole system was designed to humiliate the prisoners, break their spirit, and limit their powers of resistance. Prisoners' personal possessions were taken away and their heads were shaved. They wore uniforms and were given a number by which they would be known. The SS aimed to destroy any unity there may have been among the prisoners. They appointed block leaders and KAPOS from among the ranks of the prisoners. They were responsible for keeping order. The kapos received privileges in return. Often they were as cruel as the SS guards. The Jews were treated with particular harshness, and thousands of Soviet prisoners of war were systematically shot in the camps.

Third phase, 1942–1945. Once they began to lose the war, the Nazis desperately needed to produce more arms. They used FORCED LABOR from the concentration camps to this end. At the same time, however, the Nazi state was following its policy of murder against its so-called racial enemies: "the Jews, Slavs, and Gypsies." The Auschwitz camp, for example, had both aims. It used large numbers of slave laborers in local factories and at the same time murdered "racial enemies" in the GAS CHAMBERS. In October 1942, the central administration for SS economic activities (which had become responsible for overseeing the camps in March 1942) ordered that all concentration camps on German soil should be rid of Jews. Jewish prisoners were then sent to Auschwitz and Majdanek.

In the later stages of the war, the SS sold large numbers of workers to German companies (to replace workers who were drafted into the army) and made huge profits. During these years, the SS did not build new large camps. However, existing camps were expanded and satellite camps set up around them. DORA-MITTELBAU, which had been a satellite of Buchenwald, became an independent camp in 1944, and BERGEN-BELSEN was taken over in 1943 and gradually included in the camp system.

Estimates of the number of people killed in the concentration camps are difficult to make, but they range from 700,000 to over 1,000,000. SS figures for January 1945 gave 714,211 prisoners alive in the camps. Many of these died in the last months of the war, as concentration camps were closed down and prisoners sent on DEATH MARCHES.

COUNCIL FOR AID TO JEWS

see ZEGOTA.

COWARD, CHARLES

(1904–) British soldier who, as a prisoner of war, helped Jews in AUSCHWITZ. As a sergeant-major in the British artillery, Coward was sent to FRANCE at the outbreak of WORLD WAR II. Two weeks later, he was taken prisoner by the Nazis. He made 19 daring escapes from numerous prison camps, but each time he was recaptured. Finally, he was sent to the

> *Charles Coward devised an unusual plan for helping Jewish slave laborers to escape. On a visit to Auschwitz he bribed a prison-guard to "sell" him dead Jews and deposit the bodies in a ditch near the camp. The payment would be ten bars of chocolate and twenty cigarettes. It was agreed that Coward would receive three dead Jews. Coward then sent a message to a Jewish prisoner that he and two friends should hide in the ditch on their way back from work patrol. There they would find civilian clothes and have a chance to escape. Coward and an accomplice then went to the ditch and dragged the corpses back to the road. A search party from Auschwitz discovered the three bodies on the road and decided that these must be the missing Jews who apparently collapsed and died on their way back from work. Coward's scheme had succeeded: over 100 Jews are believed to have been saved this way.*

Monowitz prisoner of war camp in POLAND, a little more than a mile from Auschwitz-Birkenau. From Monowitz he could see the endless stream of cargo trains bringing Jews to the GAS CHAMBERS and crematoria. Because of his rank, Coward was able to secure the position of liaison officer between the prison camp authorities and the RED CROSS. This gave him access to Red Cross rations, which he sometimes used to bribe guards and enter Auschwitz. It is believed that he managed to help over 100 Jews to escape. After the war, Coward returned to England. He served as a witness in several TRIALS OF WAR CRIMINALS. In 1967, a tree was planted in his honor in YAD VASHEM's Avenue of the "RIGHTEOUS AMONG THE NATIONS."

CRACOW

see KRAKÓW.

CREMATORIA

see GAS CHAMBERS.

CRIMES AGAINST HUMANITY

A new legal category of crimes that was developed to include the atrocities committed by the Nazis and Japanese during WORLD WAR II. No specific international law existed that defined the Nazi murders

> Definition of Crimes against Humanity in the Charter of the International Military Tribunals, which tried Nazi war criminals:
>
> *Murder, extermination, enslavement, deportation and other inhumane acts committed against any civilian population, before or during the war, or persecution on political, racial or religious grounds in execution of or in connection with any crimes within the jurisdiction of the tribunal, whether or not in violation of the domestic law of the country where they were perpetrated.*

and persecutions as a crime before this category was created. It allowed Nazis to be charged with "crimes against humanity" in the TRIALS OF WAR CRIMINALS. It also influenced the definition of GENOCIDE in the United Nations Genocide Convention. Crimes against the Jews were the worst and the most far-reaching of Nazi crimes against any group.

C R O A T I A

One of the federal republics of former YUGOSLAVIA. Once a province in the Austro-Hungarian Empire, Croatia proclaimed its independence in 1918. It later joined other provinces of the Empire to create the federal nation of YUGOSLAVIA. About half of its population were Catholics. Estimates of the number of JEWS living in Croatia before WORLD WAR II vary between 30,000 and 40,000. Most belonged to the middle classes and were fairly prosperous. They enjoyed full civic and religious rights and maintained their own religious and cultural institutions, including a number of youth movements, mainly Zionist. However, the long tradition of antisemitism existing in Croatia was reinforced by events in Nazi GERMANY. Growing demands for secession from Yugoslavia were led by the USTASHA the FASCIST, nationalist movement led by Ante PAVELIC.

Yugoslavia was invaded by the joint forces of Germany and ITALY in 1940. In April 1941, Pavelic proclaimed the independence of Croatia. Though Germany and Italy recognized the new regime, they set up garrisons in the country. Pavelic instituted a dictatorial regime. Half of the country's 2 million Serbs were killed, expelled or forcibly converted to Catholicism. Anti-Jewish laws were enacted immediately; they included a new law, based on the NUREMBERG LAWS, which deprived Jews of most of their rights. Jews and their property had to be marked by a special insignia. Heavy fines were imposed on the Jewish community. Wholesale theft of Jewish property was carried out with no restraint and an estimated 50 million dollars' worth of goods were stolen. From summer 1941 onwards, able-bodied Jews were drafted for forced labor and a number of LABOR and CONCENTRATION CAMPS were set up. Those camp inmates who were not killed by harsh conditions and deprivation were shot. However, the Croatians were not killing Jews fast enough for the Germans. Following the WANNSEE CONFERENCE (January 1942), an agreement was reached between Croatian and German authorities. Croatians would arrest the Jews and hand them over to the Germans at railroad stations and would confiscate whatever property was owned by the victims. The Croatians also paid the sum of 30 reichsmarks per Jew to cover the cost of their transport to the death camp. In August 1942, 9,000 Jews, were deported to AUSCHWITZ. Smaller groups were deported in the course of the years 1942 and 1943, including Jews who had fled to parts of the country occupied by Italian troops. Croatian acts of cruelty against Serbs and Jews were among the most barbaric committed in this era. Children were concentrated in special camps where they were gassed. An estimated 80 percent of the Jews of Croatia died.

CYPRUS DETENTION CAMPS

Detention camps established in Cyprus (an island in the eastern Mediterranean Sea) by the British, for JEWS they captured trying to enter PALESTINE without their permission.

After the Holocaust, most survivors had nowhere to go. Many, if not most, wanted to move to British-controlled Palestine, in order to rebuild their lives in a Jewish homeland. The British, however, strictly limited Jewish immigration to Palestine, for fear of offending the Arabs there. Most refugees who had fled from Europe and made their way by sea or land to Palestine were labeled "illegal." The journey was dangerous, but even so, large numbers of Jewish survivors attempted it. This often meant fleeing through the mountains of Europe, being smuggled across borders, and arriving at a Mediterranean port city to board secretly a ship for Palestine (see ALIYA BET).

As a means of stopping the growing immigration of refugees, the British government decided, on 7 August 1946, to imprison "illegal" Jewish immigrants in Cyprus. As the refugee ships approached the port of Haifa in Palestine, British soldiers informed the passengers that they would be deported to Cyprus. The Holocaust survivors suffered tremendous frustration at seeing the Land of Israel, but not being allowed to enter. This often led to

Overcrowded housing in tin huts in the Derelia detention camp in Cyprus to which the British sent Holocaust survivors trying to enter Palestine without entry certificates from 1946 to 1949

violent clashes with British troops. Despite the clashes and deportations to Cyprus, immigration attempts continued.

The first Cyprus detention camp was opened on 14 August 1946, with the arrival of the ship *Yagur* (which sailed from FRANCE to Palestine on 29 July 1946 with 754 passengers, mainly Polish Jews). Within a three-year period, over 50,000 Jews were detained in Cyprus, taken from 39 boats that were blocked from landing in Palestine. Over 80 percent of the detainees were young, between the ages 13 and 35; 2,200 children were born in the detention camps.

The British army ran the camp according to regulations made for prisoner of war camps. Conditions were harsh, although better than life in the Nazi camps. Overcrowded housing was in tents or tin huts. Inmates suffered from limited food of low quality, lack of clothing and poor sanitary conditions. Water was rationed. Jewish medical and welfare teams from Palestine ran clinics and provided basic services to the inmates.

Jews from Palestine also set up an educational system in Cyprus. Most of the young people were involved in a sort of youth camp. Here many received, in addition to schooling, secret military training for future service in a Jewish army in Palestine.

Adults and youth prepared for their future resettlement in Palestine by studying Hebrew, Jewish history, and Jewish customs. There were also theater and dance groups, choirs, and athletic events. Zionist political parties were active in the camps.

Since the number of inmates kept growing, the British decided at the end of 1946 to grant 750 visas a month for Palestine. With each monthly departure of 750 people, there were public celebrations.

The largest celebration came on 29 November 1947, when the United Nations (UN) voted to partition Palestine, and set up a Jewish state. The internees in Cyprus had cabled a demand for partition, which was read aloud at the UN.

The sovereign Jewish State of ISRAEL was declared on 14 May 1948. Gradually, the prisoners departed, but it took nine months—until 10 February 1949—before the last group left Cyprus for Israel.

CZECHOSLOVAKIA

Central European republic, formed in 1918, which united the Czech and Slovak nations. Following the MUNICH AGREEMENT of September 1938, Adolf HITLER occupied the predominantly German western border areas known as the Sudetenland. What was left of the Czech Republic existed only between

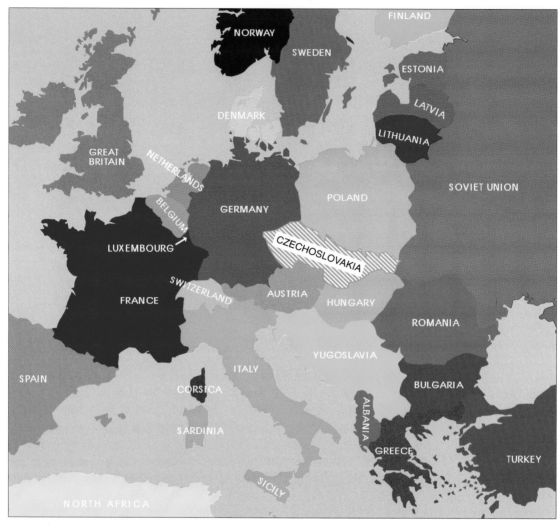

September 1938 and March 1939, when the Germans invaded.

After the Munich Agreement, President Eduard Benes resigned and was succeeded by the Supreme Court judge Emil Hácha. A two-party system was introduced. The new government, however, was plagued by both internal and international problems, among them the "Jewish Question." In addition, both POLAND and HUNGARY made claims on Czechoslovak land while radical separatists in SLOVAKIA demanded independence. Thus, this attempt at a model democracy of Central Europe was divided into a state with three separate governments: Czech, Slovak and Ruthene. (Ruthenia was a region of central Europe which had been incorporated into Czechoslovakia).

Throughout the period, following the Munich Agreement Hitler, who intended to overrun Czechoslovakia, took advantage of the conflicts between groups in the region. Nazi propaganda was distributed by agents planted in the area who took every opportunity to incite anti-Jewish feelings. Antisemitism grew when Jewish refugees arrived from the Sudetenland. While right-wing groups voiced strong anti-Jewish sentiment and many called for the expulsion of Jewish refugees, the official government position was to accept Jews fleeing from the various European countries. Due to Czechoslovakia's location at the crossroads of Europe and its reputation as a highly democratic country, it became a haven for anti-Nazi exiles. The Czech capital, PRAGUE, became a transit center for Jews from the region who were awaiting foreign visas.

The Jewish leadership of Czechoslovakia made supreme efforts, both monetarily and socially, to aid these refugees. A number of relief agencies

Jewish property being removed in Prague, Czechoslovakia

were founded with money from various private sources and foreign organizations. Despite this effort, however, a deep anxiety prevailed among the Jews of Czechoslovakia. By February 1939, the conditions for Jews in the region had worsened: professors were dismissed from their posts, doctors were asked to leave public hospitals, artists were removed from their establishments and sports teams dismissed their Jewish players. Over 5,300 people applied for visas from the American consulate during the two weeks before Hitler took over.

In March 1939, the Nazis occupied the entire Czech region and declared it the German Protec-

Calendar of deportations of Jews of Czechoslovakia to Theresienstadt

torate of BOHEMIA AND MORAVIA. Slovakia was separated and pronounced independent, although it was led by a pro-Nazi puppet government. After the Germans divided the Czechoslovak state, each region followed a different path in its anti-Jewish activity.

CZERNIAKÓW, ADAM

(1880–1942) Chairman of the JUDENRAT (Jewish Council) of WARSAW.

Czerniaków was a chemical engineer by training. He was involved in political life in POLAND before the Holocaust, serving on Warsaw's Municipal Council from 1927 to 1934, and in 1931 was elected to the Polish Senate.

GERMANY invaded Poland on 1 September 1939. During the Nazi siege of Warsaw, the city's mayor asked Czerniaków to head the Jewish religious community in Warsaw. In October, the Germans ordered Czerniaków to appoint 24 members to a Judenrat and to serve as its head.

The Nazis forced Warsaw's Jews into a GHETTO in October 1940. Then, Czerniaków, like other Judenrat chairmen, was placed in the terrible position of having to provide for the needs of the Jewish population while at the same time obeying Nazi demands. He greatly expanded the Judenrat. At its height, it had 25 departments, with 6,000 workers dealing with health, welfare, culture, and education.

Czerniaków tried to use his close contacts with the Germans for the benefit of the ghetto inhabitants. This usually did not work. In fact, he was beaten up by the Nazis on two occasions while appealing to them on behalf of ghetto residents.

Many Jews criticized Czerniaków's policies as too controlling. The ghetto's historian, Emanuel RINGELBLUM, claimed that Czerniaków's close integration into Polish society background kept him from truly identifying with the Jewish people. Many of those appointed by Czerniaków to key positions in the ghetto were highly assimilated Jews. One in particular, Jewish police chief Joseph Szernyski, was a Jew who had converted to Christianity.

Unlike some other Judenrat chairmen, Czerniaków did not try to increase his authority for the sake of power alone. He also was not prepared to give in at any cost to German demands. This was shown at the start of the mass DEPORTATIONS from the Warsaw ghetto during the summer of 1942. On 22 July, Czerniakow was ordered to have Jews appear for "resettlement in the east." He knew that this meant deportation to the DEATH CAMP at TREBLINKA. This presented him with a terrible moral dilemma. He could not bring himself to select Jews for almost certain death by handing them over for deportation. Yet he knew that if the quota of 7,000 a day was not met, the entire ghetto would be destroyed. Czerniaków chose neither of these options. He chose suicide. According to a note found on his desk, Czerniaków wrote: "They are demanding that I kill the children of my people with my own hands. There is nothing for me to do but to die."

D A C H A U

German CONCENTRATION CAMP located 10 miles from Munich. It was opened in March 1933 with a capacity of 5,000 prisoners.

In February 1933, Adolf HITLER began to establish his absolute dictatorship and one of his earliest actions was to arrest political opponents. Thus, communists, Social Democrats and monarchists, all political enemies of the Nazi Party, became the first prisoners of Dachau. On 11 April, the camp was taken over by the SS. Theodore EICKE was appointed first commandant of Dachau. Under Eicke's guidance, Dachau became the general model for all concentration camps.

Following KRISTALLNACHT (November 1938) more than 10,000 Jews were sent to Dachau. At this stage, they were released if they could prove their intent to leave GERMANY. From 1942, when the "FINAL SOLUTION" began in full, Jews interned in Dachau were transported to the DEATH CAMPS in POLAND.

The Dachau camp was surrounded by a large ditch filled with water and an electrified fence. It was staffed by members of the SS DEATH'S HEAD UNITS, which were known for their savagery. Upon arrival at Dachau, prisoners were stripped of all their possessions and lost all legal rights. They were first given a number and a colored triangle indicating their prisoner category. Their heads were shaved and they were dressed in striped uniforms. They built roads, drained marshes, worked in quarries, and were hired out to private industry. In the last case, payment for labor went directly to the SS, with nothing going to the laborers. Essentially the prisoners worked this way until they became ill, at which point they were returned to the camp to be replaced by healthier people. More than 30,000 died under these conditions.

Dachau was one of the sites in which MEDICAL EXPERIMENTS were performed on prisoners. Dr. Sigmund Rascher, an SS physician, conducted decompression experiments on inmates, resulting in the deaths of 80 out of 200 human beings. He also conducted freezing experiments on 400 people; 90 died. Dr. Claus Schilling conducted experiments at Dachau, in which he infected more than 1,000 inmates with malaria.

Dachau did not have a gas chamber, but there were mass executions. From October 1941 to April 1942, large numbers of SOVIET PRISONERS OF WAR were executed on a nearby SS shooting range. Sick and weakened prisoners were systematically killed. In

Group of survivors liberated in Dachau, 1945. In the background, the crematoria where bodies were burned

General view of Dachau concentration camp

Hitler enters Danzig, on 19 September 1939

addition, on 26 April 1945, 7,000 prisoners were force-marched south by the SS, who shot those who fell behind in line. Dachau was liberated on 29 April 1945. At the time of liberation about one-third of the inmates were Jewish.

Following the war, 40 of the Dachau SS guards were captured and tried. Thirty-six were condemned to death.

DANZIG (Gdánsk)

Historic port city on the Baltic Sea, presently in POLAND.

Danzig passed from Polish to Prussian (German) rule in 1793. In 1920 it became a free city (belonging to no particular country), with the rights of minorities guaranteed by the League of Nations. In the early 1930s, there were some 9,000 Jews in Danzig (three percent of the city's inhabitants), and they played an important role in the city's trade and industry. After 1933, Danzig's largely German population increasingly fell under Nazi influence. By 1937, the Jews became the targets of violence and by

1938, 5,000 Jews had left the city. In November 1938, synagogues, Jewish businesses and private homes were attacked and looted.

Under the energetic leadership of E. Lichtenstein, the Jewish community organized the emigration of its members. Many went secretly to PALESTINE. They sent abroad the most precious religious objects and communal archives. The city's monumental synagogue was sold for a small sum and was immediately dismantled by the Nazis. On the eve of the war, about 1,600 (mainly elderly) Jews remained. Emigration of Jews continued until November 1941, when it was stopped by the Nazis (several hundred reached Palestine). Six hundred remained and they were sent to THERESIENSTADT and the Polish ghettos. Nearly all perished. About 20 Jews with non-Jewish spouses survived the war.

DARQUIER DE PELLEPOIX, LOUIS

(1897–1980) Second commissioner-general for Jewish affairs in the VICHY government.

Darquier was a committed antisemite. As early as 1937, he had said that all JEWS should be expelled from FRANCE or massacred. In 1942, he took over from Xavier VALLAT as commissioner-general for Jewish affairs. Under Darquier's leadership, persecution of the French Jewish population became even more brutal. Violent acts against Jews and seizure of Jewish property increased dramatically.

After the war, Darquier escaped to Spain, where he lived until his death. In 1978, a French journalist interviewed him at his home in Spain. In the interview, he denied his role in the persecutions of Jews. He added that the Holocaust was a lie, saying, "They only gassed lice in AUSCHWITZ."

DARRÉ, RICHARD WALTER

(1895–1953) Nazi ideologist and German Minister of Food and Agriculture from June 1933 to May 1942. Darré believed that a farming society, rooted in the soil, should replace urban industrialization. These ideas and his antisemitism were at first very attractive to Heinrich HIMMLER, and he became one of his main advisors. However, Darré's failure to achieve practical results led to his loss of influence in Nazi circles.

Darré wrote a great deal on the importance of the peasant farmer in German history. He described a mystical link between the blood of the German race and the soil. This contributed to the important Nazi concept of LEBENSRAUM (conquering more living space for GERMANY). In 1949, he was tried and sentenced to seven years' imprisonment, but was released in 1950.

Registration of Richard Walther Darré

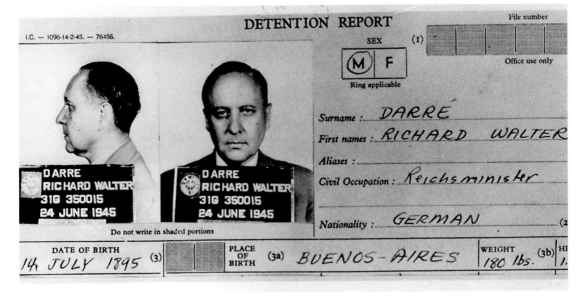

DEATH CAMPS
(Extermination Camps)

The most notorious CAMPS created by the Nazis. A death camp was a murder machine. Nearly everyone who entered it was murdered. Those who survived had either been selected to assist in the murder process or were lucky enough to be liberated before their turn came.

There were six death camps: CHELMNO, AUSCHWITZ, TREBLINKA, BELZEC, SOBIBÓR, and MAJDANEK. Each (except Chelmno) was located on a major railroad line, which made it easier to transport Jews to the death camps.

Belzec was established in March 1942 and Sobibór in May 1942. Treblinka opened in July 1942. Majdanek, near LUBLIN, was originally created to be a CONCENTRATION CAMP, but in May 1942, it was changed into a killing center. Auschwitz opened in 1940 as a concentration camp for Soviet and Polish prisoners of war (it was originally built as a Polish army camp), but in the spring of 1942, it also became a killing machine.

The first death camp to be created was Chelmno, in early December 1941. It was located in western POLAND, not far from LÓDZ. The method of killing at Chelmno was by gas vans. This was thought to be a more efficient method of murder than that which was used by the EINSATZGRUPPEN—mass murder by machine gun.

Auschwitz, located 40 miles west of Kraków, was actually a system of camps. The prisoners at Auschwitz I were mostly prisoners of war. It had a small GAS CHAMBER AND CREMATORIUM. Auschwitz II, known as Birkenau, was the death camp. It housed four large gas chambers and four crematoria. Auschwitz III, known as Buna-Monowitz, was a slave labor camp which housed the factories of I.G. FARBEN and Buna which produced synthetic rubber. In Auschwitz there were "selections." A Nazi doctor stood at the ramp as each trainload arrived and decided who would live and who would die. The young and strong were sometimes saved and used as slave laborers. The majority were "selected" for death. A million to a million and a half Jews were murdered at Auschwitz.

Treblinka, Sobibór, Belzec, and Majdanek were on the eastern border of Poland with Russia. These camps were established not only to kill the large Jewish communities of Poland, but also to help murder the Jews of the former SOVIET UNION. Sobibór, Belzec, and Treblinka were similar to each other.

Memorial Hall in Yad Vashem, Jerusalem, with names of the major camps

Crematorium preserved in Majdanek death camp

Treblinka was located 50 miles northeast of WARSAW, and Sobibór about 50 miles northeast of Lublin. Belzec was also in the Lublin district. When Jews got off the trains at Treblinka, Belzec, and Sobibór, they were hurried along a path where they were registered. Then they were sent into changing rooms and "showers." These were actually chambers of poisonous gas. No "selections" were made at these camps. Almost everyone who entered died and almost all the victims were Jewish. After the people were murdered, their bodies were dragged into huge pits, where they were burned.

In Treblinka, approximately 800,000 Jews were killed between the spring of 1942 and the summer of 1943, which made it the most efficient murder machine. In Belzec, 600,000 Jews were murdered, and in Sobibór, 250,000.

The Germans planned to make Majdanek the largest of the death camps. However, when the tide of the war changed, it was one of the first to be liberated. It was a combined death and labor camp. Many died of malnutrition, starvation, exposure or overwork, or were beaten or shot to death. Their bodies were cremated and their ashes dumped in a pile. A small gas chamber was attached to the crematoria. There were also experimental gas chambers used for determining the least amount of gas necessary to murder a certain number of people in a certain space. Approximately 125,000 Jews were murdered in Majdanek.

There were several attempts at revolts within the death camps. In Auschwitz, a gas chamber and one of the crematoria were blown up by the Jewish SON-DERKOMMANDO (those who were forced to work in the gas chambers). In Treblinka and in Sobibór, UNDER-GROUND movements attempted mass escapes.

The death camps were liberated by Soviet forces as they moved west. The Nazis, upon realizing they were soon to be invaded, sent the surviving Jews on DEATH MARCHES toward GERMANY in order to buy time and allow the German camps' staff to escape. When Allied forces arrived at the camps there were hardly any prisoners remaining. Those who had stayed behind were too weak or sick to march and had been left to die. (See AKTION REINHARD.)

DEATH MARCHES

The forced marches of Jews and others toward their deaths. They were used by the Nazis many times during the Holocaust.

The Germans began using death marches in 1941, when hundreds of thousands of SOVIET PRISONERS OF WAR were herded along the highways of the UKRAINE and BYELORUSSIA from one CAMP to another. Romanians, who were German allies, forcibly marched Jews from BESSARABIA and BUKOVINA to TRANSNISTRIA. Thousands died en route. In 1942, Jews were marched from small ghettos to larger ones, and from there sent to DEATH CAMPS.

In the fall of 1944, Adolf EICHMANN was in a hurry to deport Hungarian Jews from BUDAPEST to their deaths. On 8 November, a death march began. Almost 70,000 men, women and children were marched to the Austrian border. Many died on the way, from starvation, cold and exhaustion. The march lasted a month. Most of those who survived were sent to DACHAU and MAUTHAUSEN CONCENTRATION CAMPS.

Further death marches were the forced marches of concentration camp inmates from German-occupied POLAND toward inland GERMANY in the winter of 1944–1945. By that time, the Germans knew that the war was lost. As the Soviet army closed in, SS officials did not want eyewitnesses remaining in the camps when they were overrun. However, Germany still needed slave labor and more time to complete the "FINAL SOLUTION."

In January 1945, just days before the Red Army

We worked in a labor camp called Christianstadt near Auschwitz in an ammunition factory. In the beginning of February 1945, we were told the commandant wanted us to get all our things together and leave. We are going to walk. The Russians are behind us and we have to get away from them.... We had no idea where we were going. The commandant said, "How many there will be at the end is not my responsibility. I am just supposed to bring you." Some were shot on this walk. They couldn't walk anymore and some tried to run away and were shot and others got away.

We had civilian winter coats and we had a little square striped piece on the back of the coat. A square hole was made into the coat and it was sewn into the coat. But most of us had—for some reason—scissors and a needle and thread in the camp, so when we had a little free time, we put a piece of material from our coat underneath that hole and then sewed the striped piece back on. It just seemed like somebody had the idea and we all copied it.

As we marched my girlfriend and I were talking. There were so many women you couldn't keep track of who is missing. We made the plans at night if there was an opportunity the next day to run off, what our names would be and what we would say to people. So as we gathered again in rows of five, the two of us ran. Nobody saw us. We took our scissors and we cut off these pieces of striped material. We threw them in the brook and we sang songs. We got stopped by a policemen and he said, "Aren't you two girls from the Jewish group that went by?" and we made the attempt to look very surprised. How could he think that we would be two Jewish girls? After that we stayed with some people overnight. We told everybody that we were cousins, and we changed our names. So we went on our way and we joined a troop of German refugees and we went to the Sudetenland in Germany. Our German helped us and there we took jobs with some families.

From the testimony of Eva Gerstl Burns,
Gratz College Holocaust Oral History Archive

Death march of Dachau prisoners, April 1945

arrived at AUSCHWITZ, 66,000 prisoners were marched west to the town of Wodzislaw where they were put on freight trains to the GROSS-ROSEN, BUCHENWALD, Dachau, and Mauthausen concentration camps. Almost one in four died en route. On 20 January 1945, 7,000 Jews, 6,000 of them women, were marched from STUTTHOF's satellite camps in the Danzig region of Poland. In the course of the 10-day march, 700 were murdered. Those who remained alive when they reached the shores of the Baltic Sea were driven into the sea and shot. There were only 13 known survivors.

There were 59 different marches from Nazi concentration camps during the final winter of Nazi rule, some covering hundreds of miles. The prisoners were given little or no food or water, and hardly any time to rest or take care of bodily needs. Many reached the end of their strength and collapsed. Those who paused to rest or fell behind were shot.

DEATH'S-HEAD UNITS (SS TOTENKOPFVERBÜNDE)

Units of the SS assigned to Nazi CONCENTRATION CAMPS and also elite combat units most noted for war crimes.

The Death's-Head Units were named for the skull and cross bone emblem they wore on the right collar of their uniforms. They also wore a dark brown uniform, rather than the standard black uniform of the SS. Candidates for these units were at least 5'10" tall, between the ages of 17 and 22 and racially pure "Aryans." They were recruited from among the toughest Nazi youth and served for 12 years.

Theodor EICKE, the first commandant of DACHAU and also the first inspector of concentration camps, established the units in 1934. He aimed to develop in his men strict discipline and cruelty. They instituted a brutal regime in the Nazi concentration camp system.

By the outbreak of WORLD WAR II, the Death's-Head Units and their reserves numbered some 24,000 men, increasing to 40,000 men by January 1945. Some of the Death's-Head Units were released from concentration camp service for combat duty. In November 1939, Eicke established the Death's-Head Division. They were known for their fierce fighting,

their cruelty toward enemy soldiers and civilians, and their extremely high rate of casualties. The division was an elite SS fighting force, infamous for its savage conduct, especially in the war against SOVIET RUSSIA. The Death's-Head Division committed atrocities, chiefly against partisans and enemy soldiers.

After the war, the International Military Tribunal at Nuremberg declared the Death's-Head Units to be a criminal organization. Members of the units were subject to arrest and trial as war criminals.

DE GAULLE, CHARLES

((1890–1970) French military general and political leader. De Gaulle was the head of the Free French Movement in ALGERIA and London during WORLD WAR II (see GOVERNMENTS-IN-EXILE).

When the Germans invaded FRANCE in May 1940 and the French army crumbled, he was bitterly opposed to the idea of surrendering to the Nazis. He proposed that if the need arose, the government should withdraw to North Africa, and continue the war against Nazism from there. He escaped to London after the fall of France in June 1940. From there he called on all those who did not accept Marshal PÉTAIN's armistice agreement with the Nazis to join him in forming the Free French Movement. In June 1941, he fought the VICHY forces in Syria and

General Charles de Gaulle (right), Prime Minister Winston Churchill (center) and General Wladyslaw Sikorski, the prime minister of the Polish government-in-exile (left) in Great Britain

General De Gaulle's victory march along Champs Elysée after the liberation of Paris, August 1944

Lebanon to free those French colonies from Nazi occupation. After the Allies drove the Germans out of North Africa in 1942–1943, de Gaulle was eventually put in charge (May 1943) and three months later he canceled Pétain's ANTI-JEWISH LEGISLATION in Algeria and placed that country under the control of the Free French.

As leader of the Free French, de Gaulle directed the forces of the resistance in Nazi-occupied and Vichy France. He shared in the victory when the Germans were driven out of France in July 1944 and he returned in triumph.

De Gaulle became prime minister of the temporary French government that was established when PARIS was liberated in August 1944. He undertook measures to cancel all racial laws and return rights and possessions to the Jews. From 1958 to 1969, he was president of the French Republic.

DENAZIFICATION

Process introduced by the Allies after WORLD WAR II to rid GERMANY of Nazi rule and punish Nazi officials. Even before the war ended, Allied leaders declared that it was their aim to destroy the NAZI PARTY. They would cancel its laws, destroy its institutions, and re-move Nazi Party officials from their posts (see box).

Denazification was a huge task. Formal programs were put into place to remove Nazi sympathizers from all areas of life. Not only government and army officials, but teachers, administrators, and lawyers were investigated. Well-known Nazis, usually those involved in politics on the national level, were subject to mandatory arrest and placed in internment camps. A great number of people in local leadership

Nazis must be completely and finally removed from all aspects of German life. The Nazi Party and its affiliated agencies must be utterly destroyed. Active Nazis and militants, and their ardent supporters must be removed from positions of influence in any part of the German community. Nazi teachings and doctrines must be wiped out. War criminals must be tried and punished as they deserve.

directive from the U.S. Chiefs of Staff, late summer, 1945 positions, however, were never put under arrest.

In October 1946, the Allies issued a joint statement that named five categories of Nazis: Major Offenders; Offenders; Lesser Offenders; Followers; and Persons Exonerated (found not to be Nazis). Individuals had to complete a questionnaire that asked them about membership in the Nazi Party, military service, employment, and other aspects of their lives. These statements were examined by a panel of Allied military or local German government officials. The panel decided on a punishment, ranging from arrest to a fine. People who fell into the first three categories were generally banned from running in elections for a limited period. However, many people lied in their questionnaires. Thus, in reality, most officials were exonerated or let off lightly as "Followers." The system was complicated, had many loopholes, and was largely considered unfair. By 1948, many "Offenders" were able to start climbing back into positions of power in German society.

After the war, Germany was divided into four zones. Each was run by one of the Allied powers (the UNITED STATES, GREAT BRITAIN, SOVIET RUSSIA, and FRANCE). Each zone carried out denazification to a different degree. Denazification was first introduced and most strictly applied in the American zone. In the British zone, compromises were made. The zone had a large population and it was the most badly bombed. The British authorities decided that in order to rebuild the economy they would have to keep some Nazis in important positions. They therefore compromised on denazification principles to keep local Nazi experts in their jobs. The French also did not strictly enforce the policy. In the Soviet zone, denazification was used to set up communist regimes. Nazi leaders accused of war crimes (see UNITED NATIONS WAR CRIMES COMMISSION) were arrested and Nazi industrialists had their businesses and money seized by the state. However, if local officials could show that they were willing to work toward a communist society, they were allowed to stay at their posts.

With the beginning of the cold war (the postwar rivalry between the United States and Soviet Russia), less attention was given to denazification by the Allies. By 1948, the process was handed over to the German authorities, except in the Soviet zone, where it was ended altogether.

DENIAL OF THE HOLOCAUST

see HOLOCAUST, DENIAL OF THE.

DENMARK

Scandinavian country bordered by GERMANY on the south. JEWS were first invited to settle in Denmark in 1622. They received Danish citizenship in 1814 and full rights in 1849. The total Jewish population has

---

The Danish fishermen took you over but you had to pay, and I had nothing. So the ones who could pay more got in first, and the ones who didn't pay anything had to sneak themselves aboard. I got on a herring boat, a little tiny boat, and there were 25 of us. We go into the hull of the ship and they cover us up and we are sailing and sailing for ten hours and we are getting nowhere. This fisherman did not have a map. He didn't have a compass. He just sailed according to the stars. We wound up on the Polish side of the Kattegat and the Germans came on board the ship—the German soldiers with their bayonets. There was herring on top of the tarpaulin and we were underneath. They were walking on top and your heart was in your throat. To this day, I think that the Germans must have known that we were there. They ordered the fisherman back to Denmark but we got to Sweden eventually. It was 22 hours later.

Suddenly, you see the coast. We didn't know if it was the Danish coast, the Swedish coast, the Polish coast, and suddenly we see all of these little rowboats coming out to us, rowing out to us and waving. The Swedes came over in the rowboats and they took us in. We didn't even know where we landed, what town, and we all just cried and laughed. It was like seeing the Promised Land.

From the testimony of Hanna Seckel-Drucker, Gratz College Holocaust Oral History Archive

been stable at 6,000 for most of this century. The rate of intermarriage in Denmark is among the highest in the world.

The story of Denmark in the Holocaust period involves three time periods. The first, from 1934 to 1940, corresponds with the spread of Nazism in Europe leading up to the German occupation. During these years, Denmark's policies toward foreign Jewish refugees was similar to those of other European states. Immigration laws gave preference to political refugees. This policy tended to have disastrous consequences for Jews since it excluded them. By the end of this period, the estimated 4,500 Jews who succeeded in escaping to Denmark had left the country. Non-Scandinavians found it very difficult to find employment.

The second period began on 9 April 1940, when Germany occupied Denmark. The Danes collabo-

rated in an unusual way. They were able to continue administering their own national affairs by not offering any real military resistance to the Nazis. They carried on a "policy of negotiation" with the Germans and reached an agreement whereby the occupiers would not harm the Jews or their property. Apparently, the "Jewish question" was debated publicly in early 1942—about the same time as the "FINAL SOLUTION" was beginning to be put into practice elsewhere in Europe. The Danes reached public consensus that it was a national, ethical imperative to preserve the liberty of all its citizens without discrimination. Nazi efforts to sway the feelings of the local population against the Jews were ineffective. The Jews of Denmark were safe.

The third period began on 28 August 1942 when the Danish-German Agreement was abolished and the Danish government resigned. With the

lasted for three weeks, with the full support of the Danish people. It involved all elements of Danish society—from King Christian X to the various churches, the students, and the resistance. All tolled, 7,200 Jews and 700 of their non-Jewish relatives were saved.

Fewer than 500 Jews had been arrested on the night of October 1. They were sent to THERESIENSTADT. Danish support for their country's endangered Jews did not stop at this point. The Danish Foreign Ministry led the fight to save their lives. A delegation from Denmark and another from the International Red Cross insisted on visiting the prisoners. Protests were lodged and food parcels were sent. Danish efforts to intercede at a Nazi CONCENTRATION CAMP were successful when those of others consistently failed during the Holocaust period. The Danish Jews imprisoned at Theresienstadt were not deported to Auschwitz. In fact, their freedom was negotiated before the end of the war. In total, less than 2 percent of Denmark's Jewish population perished during the Holocaust. Through the remarkable efforts of the Danish people, Jews returning from Sweden at the end of the war even found their property intact.

DEPORTATIONS

Soon after GERMANY invaded POLAND in September 1939, the Germans began the process of taking Jews from their homes and concentrating them in

Danish fishermen ferry a boatload of Jewish fugitives across a narrow sound to safety in neutral Sweden, 1943

establishment of a German military government, Denmark was essentially no different from any other occupied country. Werner BEST, the Nazi military commander in Denmark, called for the immediate deportation of the Jews. On the night of 1 October 1943, the arrests began.

The Danish reaction, however, was unique. In a spontaneous show of support, the Danish population organized a massive sea operation to evacuate the country's Jews to SWEDEN. Sweden had remained neutral and its government had offered to accept all of Denmark's refugees. The ensuing rescue operation

In accordance with official instructions of 22 July, 1942, all persons not employed in institutions or enterprises will definitely be resettled.

Forcible removals are being continued uninterruptedly. I call once more on all members of the population subject to resettlement to report voluntarily at the railway siding, and will extend for three days, including August 2, 3, and 4, 1942, the distribution of 7 pounds of bread and 2 pounds of marmalade to every person who reports voluntarily.

Director of the Order Service,
Warsaw, August 1, 1942

Cartoon by David Low from World War II

Hungarian police deporting Jews from the town of Köszeg to the Auschwitz death camp

Deportation of Jews from Wloclawek, Poland, to the Majdanek death camp

districts and ghettos. This was the first stage of deportation. The first major operation was the transfer of Jews from AUSTRIA, CZECHOSLOVAKIA and elsewhere to the NISKO AND LUBLIN reservation in Poland.

Reinhard HEYDRICH called a meeting in January 1940 to discuss the various methods of deporting Jews in the GENERALGOUVERNEMENT (puppet government of Germany within Poland). Adolf EICHMANN, who was acting as Heinrich HIMMLER's direct agent for the deportation of Jews to the East, also attended. At the meeting, it was decided to move 350,000 Jews by train to ghettos in Poland. The conditions on these trains were atrocious—hundreds of Jews were packed tightly into cattle cars. It was reported that in one of the early train transports, hundreds of Jews froze to death while being deported to ghettos.

The next stage of deportations, beginning in 1942, was the movement of Jews from ghettos into DEATH CAMPS. JUDENRAT leaders were responsible for assembling the Jews in each ghetto and for filling Nazi quotas for "relocation to the East"— another way of saying transfer to an extermination camp. Jews were deported from the ghettos, and were rounded up throughout Europe, wherever Germans were in control.

Deportations differed depending on their place of origin. The Jews of WARSAW and many other ghettos were stuffed into cattle cars and deported to TREBLINKA. The Jews of northern Europe paid for their own passage to camps, many even choosing to upgrade their fares to first-class passage. Volunteers for deportation were sometimes promised extra food if they presented themselves at the UMSCHLAG-PLATZ (the place of deportation from the ghetto). The volunteers would then hand over these rations to the remaining families as they registered and boarded the trains.

Nazi fanaticism was so strong that even as their "empire" was crashing around them, they continued to deport Jews to death camps. In seven weeks during the summer of 1944, almost 500,000 Hungarian Jews were deported to their deaths.

DER STÜRMER

see STÜRMER, DER.

DIARIES, HOLOCAUST

Personal accounts written by victims of the Holocaust. Diaries are especially valuable to historians. They offer a view that is very immediate, unlike memoirs that are written after the war. Daily entries can provide a wealth of detail on the routine of life during the Holocaust. Diaries often describe the feelings of the author and the atmosphere of the time. They give an authentic account of the way in which the writer experienced the situation he or she was in.

Individuals wrote diaries for different reasons. Some wrote of their experiences for the historical record, to give testimony for the future. Others used their diary as a "friend" to confide in. They wrote to express their feelings at a time of frightening and humiliating treatment by the Nazis. Another group of writers saw keeping a diary as an act of defiance,

Original diary of Holocaust survivor, Aba Gefen

a way of resisting the oppression forced upon them. In Nazi-occupied areas, it was a dangerous activity for a Jew to keep a diary. The penalty for being caught could be death, so the notes had to be hidden carefully. Many more diaries must have been lost during the war than those that have survived.

Diaries written by children and teenagers are among some of the most moving documents of the Holocaust. These personal memoirs serve as impressive testimonies of the experiences of young people during a dark and inhumane time. The diaries reveal how these children struggled to find meaning and understanding in a world that once felt safe, but had now turned evil and seemed hopeless. There are diaries that were kept by children in hiding, children in the GHETTOS, and children in CONCENTRATION CAMPS. Each of these has an enormous value as historic documentation of the Holocaust's complexities.

The most famous Holocaust diary was written by Anne FRANK. She described how she and her family were hidden from the Nazis in Amsterdam. This moving document of a girl in her early teens was left behind when the family was eventually betrayed and sent to their deaths. The diary was rescued by a family friend and published after the war by Anne's father, the only member of the Frank family to survive.

Other diaries written by children have also survived but are less well known. To name just a few: Mary Berg, a 15-year-old girl, wrote of the horrors of the WARSAW ghetto; Yitzhak Rudashevski docu-

> I am idle all day long and have nothing to do. I read a lot but this does not cheer me up. I feel that I am sinking lower and lower. I have tried to study the Bible but I am unable to concentrate. I shall try to borrow a volume of the Talmud. It is because I hate being idle that I have started this diary so that I can write in it every day what I do and think; in this matter I shall be able to account for all I have done each day.
>
> *from the opening entry in*
> *Moshe Flinker's diary*
> *(Young Moshe's Diary)*

mented his life in the VILNA ghetto in LITHUANIA; Eva Heyman, aged 13, described life in HUNGARY under Nazi rule in 1944; and Moshe Flinker, a religious 16-year-old, wrote in Hebrew of life in Brussels (published as *Young Moshe's Diary*).

Tamarah Lazerson was 13 years old in 1941, when the Nazis occupied her hometown of KOVNO, Lithuania, and forced the JEWS of Kovno into a ghetto. In the ghetto, Tamarah kept a diary and recorded with deep emotion the horrors of her time there. She writes in one entry:

I see the horrible devastation of war and hear the weeping of children. O my people Israel! I can't forget you. An inner voice calls me to you. I am coming. I am ready to crawl on my knees and kiss your sacred soil. Only tell me you hear my call.

Werner Galnik was eight years old in 1941, when he and his family were deported from Germany to the RIGA ghetto in Latvia, and later to two concentration camps. He wrote about his experiences in the ghetto and then in the camps.

The original diary of Anne Frank, kept in the Anne Frank House, Amsterdam

Some Holocaust Diaries

A. Czerniakow, *The Warsaw Diary of Adam Czerniakow* (New York, 1979).

Flinker, *Young Moshe's Diary* (Jerusalem 1965).

A. Frank, *A Diary of a Young Girl* (New York, 1967).

A. Gefen, *Hope in Darkness* (Jerusalem 1977).

E. Heyman, *The Diary of Eva Heyman* (Jerusalem 1976).

L. Holliday, *Children's Wartime Diaries* (London, Piatkus, 1995).

C. Kaplan, *Scroll of Agony* (New York, Macmillan, 1966).

H. Levy-Hass, *Inside Belsen* (Brighton, Harvester, 1962).

A. A. Lewin, *A Cup of Tears: A Diary of the Warsaw Ghetto* (London, Blackwell, 1990).

E. Ringelblum, *Notes from the Warsaw Ghetto: The Journal of Emanuel Ringelblum* (New York, Schocken Books, 1974).

D. Rubinowicz, *The Diary of David Rubinowicz* (Edmonds, Washington, 1982).

All of these writings and diary entries give us insight into how children lived with, and survived, trauma through first person accounts of their lives. Keeping diaries helped some children to maintain a sense of order and sanity and, in doing so, helped them to resist oppression in their hearts and minds.

A significant number of adult diaries have been preserved from the ghettos. Most of those that survived were written by persons who were involved in the Jewish administration of the ghettos. Together, they give us a detailed picture of daily life in the ghettos. They also record the personal reactions of the writers to the situation in the ghettos as the Nazis began to deport large numbers of Jews to the DEATH CAMPS. The diary of Avraham Tory, secretary of the Jewish Council (JUDENRAT) in the Kovno ghetto, documents the period from June 1941 to January 1944. Adam CZERNIAKÓW, who was the chairman of the Warsaw Jewish Council, kept a diary from 6 September 1939. It ends on 23 July 1942, just before he took his own life in despair at the DEPORTATIONS of ghetto residents to TREBLINKA. These accounts allow us to understand something of the awful dilemma of these leaders, who were forced to respond to German demands and at the same time work for the survival of their Jewish communities. The journal by the historian Emanuel RINGELBLUM is also from the Warsaw ghetto. Together with a team of researchers, Ringelblum collected information and wrote commentaries about Jewish life in the ghetto. Another major diary that has survived from the Warsaw ghetto is by Chaim Aaron KAPLAN, principal of a Hebrew school. In LÓDZ a journal of daily life and events in the ghetto was recorded by a team of people who worked for the Jewish Council.

Opportunities for keeping diaries in the concentration camps were fewer, but some people did manage to write and preserve notes. Those in the best position to keep a diary were prisoners who held administrative positions in the camps. They had access to paper and had occasional privacy. Emil Buege, who as a prisoner worked as an interpreter, was successful in keeping a diary in SACHSEN-HAUSEN. He also managed to smuggle his notes out of the camp. Hanna Levy-Hass wrote a journal while a prisoner in BERGEN-BELSEN. She vividly described the misery that she and her fellow prisoners were forced to endure. Some of the most striking of the camp diaries were those written by members of the SONDERKOMMANDO in Birkenau. These were prisoners who were forced to work in the GAS CHAMBERS AND CREMATORIA. The diaries express the full horror of their daily existence and serve as a lasting condemnation of the Nazis' racial policies.

DIBELIUS, OTTO

(1880–1967) German anti-Nazi Protestant Church leader. Dibelius was a high official in the Evangelical (Lutheran) Church. At first, he was sympathetic to the Nazis when they came to power. In a broadcast to the United States in April 1933, he excused the Nazi boycott of the Jews (see BOYCOTT, ANTI-JEWISH), saying that it was an answer to anti-Nazi protests

However, in the years that followed, he joined the Confessing Church, founded by his friend Martin NIEMÖLLER. The two men wrote a pamphlet attacking the Nazis for trying to force the CHURCHES to adopt their views. In 1937, Dibelius issued a criticism of the state for interfering in matters that belonged to religion. He was arrested, but the judges refused to bow to government pressure and acquitted him. During WORLD WAR II, he continued to protest Nazi restrictions on the churches. He was frequently arrested and forbidden to preach. Although he was aware of the killing of the Jews, he failed to protest this aspect of Nazi policy.

DISPLACED PERSONS (DPs)

At the end of WORLD WAR II there were millions of people in Europe—as much as a tenth of the population of the continent—who had been driven out of their homes by the Nazis. As the war ended, most of these people found their way back to their countries and began to rebuild their lives. With the Jewish survivors, however, it was different. After their terrible experiences, most wanted to leave the blood-soaked continent of Europe altogether and make a fresh start elsewhere. Others returned to where they came from, only to discover that their homes and possessions had been taken over by former neighbors, who had no intention of restoring the Jews' property and were hostile to the returnees. Even so, some Jews did begin to settle back in their home towns. However, following the KIELCE pogrom of 1946, in which Holocaust survivors were slaughtered by a Polish mob, many of the Jews who had returned realized there would be no future for them in Eastern Europe. They fled westward.

Thus, there were vast numbers of Jewish survivors with nowhere to go. They came to be housed in DP camps, many of which were actually located in the very vicinities of the CAMPS where they had suffered such horrors. The DP camps were located mostly in those areas of GERMANY controlled by the western Allies—especially the UNITED STATES and GREAT BRITAIN. A sincere effort was made by the armies of these countries to assist the pathetic survivors, but their plight seemed to have no solution. With few exceptions, the countries of the world would not let them in. Entrance to PALESTINE, where nearly all of them wanted to go, was closed by the British. By 1946, 250,000 Jews were packed into DP camps.

Inside the camps, a whole culture developed. The

Children studying Hebrew in a Displaced Persons' camp in Germany

activities and creativity of the inmates were outstanding examples of how the human spirit can overcome the worst disasters. People married and had children.

Education programs ranged from kindergartens to "People's Universities." Jewish festivals were observed; newspapers were published; political

Zionist demonstrators from the Landsberg Displaced Persons' camp demanding an end to British restrictions, which limited Jewish immigration into Palestine, 1945

parties were established; and theaters and orchestras were formed.

At the same time, the existence of these camps was a festering sore in the middle of Europe and a challenge to the world's conscience. United States President Harry S. TRUMAN proposed that 100,000 DPs be moved to Palestine. However, the British government was fearful of upsetting the Arabs, so it refused. Some DPs were smuggled out by Jews from Palestine and managed to get past the British block-ade to reach Palestine in the "illegal" immigration (see ALIYA BET). Those caught by the British were sent to detention camps in CYPRUS. The plight of the DPs so moved the Jews in Palestine that they re-volted against the British in order to allow immigra-tion. The British finally referred the issue to the United Nations. There a proposal was passed to di-vide Palestine into two parts, and create a Jewish state in one half. Many nations supported the pro-posal out of sympathy for the DPs. They also felt guilty about what had happened in the HOLOCAUST and for their own failure to admit the REFUGEES. Once the State of ISRAEL was established in 1948, the majority of the DPs in camps in Germany and Cyprus were at last able to find a home. The United States also finally relaxed its regulations by special Act of Congress and allowed 80,000 DPs to reach America. The problem of the displaced persons was solved.

DOCUMENTATION CENTERS

see CENTRE DE DOCUMENTATION JUIVE CONTEMPORAINE; UNITED STATES HOLOCAUST MEMORIAL MUSEUM; YAD VASHEM.

D Ö N I T Z ,   K A R L

(1891–1980) Commander of the German navy. He was one of very few members of the German High Command who really believed in Adolf HITLER and his National Socialism (most considered Hitler to be an upstart corporal). He proved his ability as a naval commander in 1939, when he developed the "pack system," in which German submarines grouped together to attack British ships. In 1942, Dönitz was promoted to admiral, and in 1943, he replaced Erich Raeder as grand admiral of the Ger-man navy. Although the development of radar made

Karl Dönitz

the pack system obsolete, Dönitz is believed to have been responsible for sinking some 15 million tons of ships manned by sailors of the Allies..

On 30 April 1945, just hours before committing suicide, Hitler appointed Dönitz as his successor. Although defeat was unavoidable, Dönitz set up a government in Flensburg Mürwick in northern GER-MANY and attempted to oversee the surrender of Germany to the British (he was terrified of what would happen if Germany fell to the Soviets). On 7 May, Germany surrendered, bringing an end to the war in Europe and to the Holocaust. Dönitz was captured on 23 May 1945.

At the war crimes TRIALS in Nuremberg, Dönitz was acquitted of "crimes against humanity." However, in 1942, he had handed the crew of a captured tor-pedo boat over to the SS and they were shot. Hitler's heir was sentenced to 10 years imprison-ment for war crimes and crimes against peace.

D O R A - M I T T E L B A U

CONCENTRATION CAMP in the Harz mountains in eastern GERMANY. It was built in 1943 as a satellite camp of

LIVING CONDITIONS IN TUNNELS OF DORA

FROM AUGUST 1943 UNTIL MARCH 1944

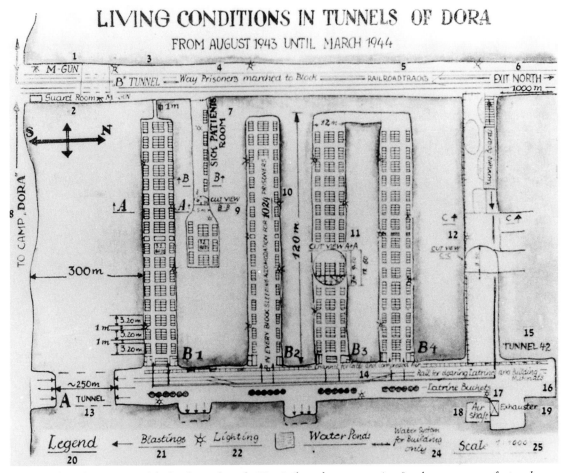

Tunnels plan of Dora, part of the bunkers where the V2 missile rockets sent against London were manufactured

BUCHENWALD. By the end of 1944, it had grown tremendously and became an independent camp, with sub-camps of its own. The inmates were all slave laborers who worked in underground factories. They built secret weapons (including V-1 and V-2 rockets), which the Germans hoped would help them win the war.

The first 10,000 prisoners to arrive there had to dig huge tunnels to house the factories. They were worked to death in appalling conditions. They lived and worked underground and were not able to breathe fresh air. They did not receive adequate water and food supplies. When prisoners died, they were replaced by other slave laborers. When the factories began production in 1944, barracks were built above ground but the laborers were still forced to work for 12 hours every day. A crematorium (see GAS CHAMBERS, GAS VANS, AND CREMATORIA) was

built in 1944 to cope with the many who died. Deaths among the Jewish prisoners were especially high since they were treated most brutally. When they were too exhausted to work, the JEWS were sent to other camps to be killed.

There was an active RESISTANCE group among the prisoners at Dora-Mittelbau. It succeeded in sabotaging the work in the armaments factories. The penalties for being caught, however, were high: many were shot or hanged.

There were over 32,000 prisoners in the main camp and sub-camps of Dora-Mittelbau at any one time during the winter of 1944. When the camp was liberated by the U.S. army on 9 April 1945, most of the starving and diseased prisoners had been transferred to BERGEN-BELSEN. They continued to die there. In 1947, an American military court tried 19 former members of the camp staff and sentenced the camp commander, Hans Karl Moeser, to death.

DRAENGER, SHIMSHON AND TOVA

Leaders of the Jewish underground in POLAND.

Shimshon Draenger (1914–1943) was born in KRAKÓW. There he became a leader of Akiva, a Zionist youth movement. Tova Draenger (1917–1943) (born Gusta Dawidson), was also born in Kraków. She was also a leader in the Akiva youth organization, which is where they met. Together with Shimshon she edited the Akiva newspaper, *Tze'irim* ("Youth").

On 22 September 1939, just three weeks after the German invasion of Poland, Shimshon and his future wife Tova were arrested for publishing articles written by anti-Nazis. They were both sent to the prison camp in Troppau, CZECHOSLOVAKIA (then part of GERMANY), and released three months later. They went to WARSAW and led an underground Akiva cell, which was disguised as an educational organization. Shimshon and Tova also ran a Zionist agricultural training farm to prepare young JEWS for a future lives as farmers in the Land of Israel.

Shimshon and Tova married in early 1940. At an early stage in the war, they called for rescue and RESISTANCE as a means of saving Jews from the Nazis. In August 1942, during the mass DEPORTATIONS from the Warsaw GHETTO to the DEATH CAMP at TREBLINKA, Shimshon and Tova helped found the PIONEER FIGHTERS *(He-Halutz ba-Lohem)*, a Jewish youth fighting organization. Shimshon was a member of its high command. He forged ghetto exit permits for its members and sold them to non-members of the organization to raise money for weapons for future resistance activities.

In January 1943, the Germans finally caught up with Shimshon. He was arrested and jailed in Warsaw's terrible Montelupich prison. Learning of her husband's arrest, Tova fulfilled a vow that she and Shimshon had made. If either of them were arrested, the other would surrender. Tova immediately turned herself over to the GESTAPO; she too was sent to Montelupich prison.

While in prison, Shimshon and Tova Draenger continued to defy the Germans—this time with spiritual resistance. Shimshon led underground

Shimshon Draenger

study sessions. Tova wrote a diary, which mostly describes their resistance activities.

Shimshon and Tova escaped from prison on 29 April 1943. They soon became PARTISAN fighters in the forests. Shimshon continued his underground educational and youth activities. Through his UNDERGROUND publication, he appealed to ghetto residents to escape to the forests—and to Jewish youth to stay in the forests and fight.

The Draengers managed to hide in the forests for half a year. Shimshon was caught by the Germans—for the last time—on 8 November 1943. Again, keeping her vow to always be united with her husband, Tova turned herself over to the Gestapo the following day. Shimshon and Tova were most probably murdered, since they were never heard from again.

Fifteen of the twenty pages of the diary Tova kept in prison were preserved and published, under the title *Justina's Diary*. It tells about the Draengers and the resistance activities of their fellow youth movement comrades—activities that Tova called "the daring revolt of the young fighters."

D R A N C Y

Site of a concentration camp in a northeastern suburb of PARIS.

This camp was an unfinished, horseshoe-shaped, concrete apartment complex. At first, it was used by the French authorities as a prison for communist sympathizers. After being taken over by the Germans, it was used to hold French, British, Yugoslavian, and Greek prisoners of war.

In August 1941, after a round-up of Jews in Paris, 6,000 Jewish men were brought to Drancy. Drancy became the main concentration camp for French JEWS until July 1944. They were deported from there to POLAND, where most of them were gassed to death at AUSCHWITZ.

Drancy was run entirely by French police until July 1943. At that time, Alois BRUNNER, the SS officer, took over the running of the camp. Conditions at Drancy were horrifying. Up to 50 inmates were in each room, sleeping three or four to a narrow wooden bunk. The mortality rate was high, with many deaths from malnutrition or dysentery. About 70,000 Jews were held at Drancy before being deported. Of these, some 2,000 survived the war. After the war, a monument was set up at the entrance to the camp.

D U C K W I T Z , G E O R G F E R D I N A N D

(1904–1973) German diplomat who helped to save Danish Jewry from the Holocaust. Duckwitz is one of the few Germans who was recognized as a "RIGHTEOUS AMONG THE NATIONS."

Duckwitz joined the Nazi Party early in 1932. He

Wall inscriptions by prisoners in Drancy recording the dates of their arrival and deportation

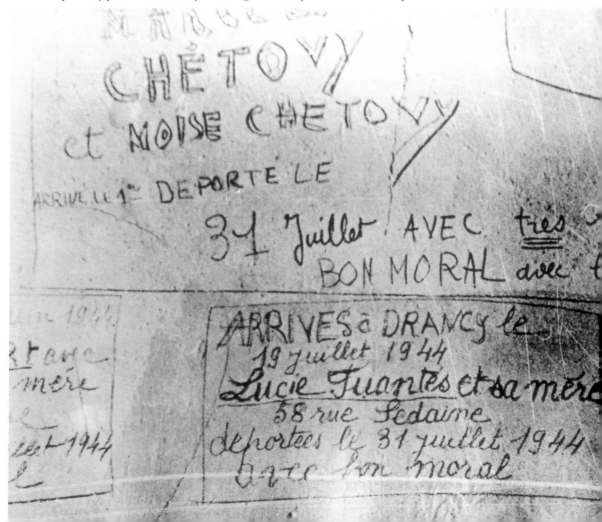

Georg Duckwitz lighting the memorial flame at a ceremony in Yad Vashem, Jerusalem. He was honored as a "Righteous among the Nations"

was sent to occupied DENMARK on behalf of German Intelligence, since he had spent several years in Copenhagen before the war. Toward the end of the summer of 1943, the Germans decided to deport the 8,000 Jews who lived in Denmark (see DEPORTATIONS). Dr. Werner BEST, chief representative of GERMANY in Denmark, told Duckwitz about the plan. Duckwitz lost no time in warning his many contacts among Danish politicians. He informed them on 28 September that Jews were to be rounded up and arrested on 1 October. Displaying remarkable solidarity and courage, the Danish people set up a rescue operation. Almost all of Danish Jewry was smuggled to safety in SWEDEN. Duckwitz was never accused or tried. After the war, he enjoyed a distinguished career in the Foreign Service of West Germany. He became director general of that ministry after serving for three years as ambassador to Copenhagen.

D U N E R A

Ship that carried refugees from GREAT BRITAIN to AUSTRALIA in 1940.

One of the United Kingdom's first steps during WORLD WAR II was to label German and Austrian na-

tionals who were residing in Britain as "enemy aliens." As a result, many Jews who had fled the Nazis to Britain were also labeled "enemy aliens." This led to restrictions on their movement. After the fall of FRANCE in 1940, some people in England thought that enemy aliens might form a "fifth column"—traitors who would support GERMANY if the Germans should invade (as had happened in some of the countries captured by Germany.) By June 1940, some 20,000 German and Austrian men—including many Jews—had been placed in internment camps.

The British government decided to send many of these detainees far away from the site of the war. They were shipped to the far reaches of the British Commonwealth, especially CANADA and AUSTRALIA. The *Dunera* set sail in September 1940. It transported some 2,400 to 2,500 "enemy aliens" to Australia. Three-quarters of them were Jews. Conditions on board were extremely bad because of crowding. The ship was designed to carry only 1,600 people. Nevertheless, the Dunera Boys, as they came to be known, decided to make the best of their situation. A number of the group's intellectuals began to give regular classes. Soon, a distinct society was taking shape. Before reaching their destination, they had even drawn up a constitution.

The act of detaining German and Austrian Jews and non-Jews together created an unusual social situation. Some of the detainees were Italian FASCISTS, and others were Nazi sympathizers. Nevertheless, when the Dunera Boys were detained in an army barracks in Hay, New South Wales, the group further developed the educational programs that had begun on the boat. Despite their restricted and basic living conditions, they set up an informal university, which offered a range of courses in the humanities and in the social and natural sciences. The detainees continued their activities when they were transferred to Tatura in Victoria.

After the war, most of the group made their homes in the United Kingdom and Australia. A large number of them later rose to important positions in universities and business. The Dunera Boys maintained a network of friendship, and have had many reunions. In the 1980s, a film called *The Dunera Boys* was produced, in which tribute was paid to the society that they had created.

e

ECLAIREURS ISRAÉLITES DE FRANCE ("French Jewish Scouts"; EIF)

French Jewish youth movement that resisted and fought the Nazis.

In May 1940, GERMANY invaded FRANCE. This put French JEWS in danger. Still, the EIF was able to function legally in southern France—the unoccupied zone—to which thousands of Jewish refugees fled. In response to this flood of refugees, the EIF set up children's homes, schools, welfare centers, and agricultural training farms. The EIF was outlawed in the occupied zone of France. Even so, it continued to function in PARIS as an UNDERGROUND movement.

The Germans began imprisoning Jews in 1941, and EIF children's homes took in the children of the prisoners. With the massive DEPORTATIONS TO POLAND of over 42,000 French Jews in the summer and fall of 1942, the EIF began a program of rescue and RESISTANCE. It established an underground rescue network called La Sixième ("The Sixth"). La Sixième provided false identity papers for children. It then either placed these children with non-Jewish families or moved them across the border to neutral SPAIN and SWITZERLAND. Several thousand Jews were saved by the EIF.

The EIF had close relations with the main Jewish fighting group, the ARMÉE JUIVE ("Jewish Army"), and also cooperated with the general French underground. La Sixième recruited thousands of volunteers for the French resistance and transmitted secret information to its members.

In early 1943, the EIF established a fighting underground organization, called the Compagnie Marc Haguenau. It was named after La Sixième leader Marc Haguenau who, after his capture by the GESTAPO, committed suicide rather than die by their hands. The Compagnie formed a unit of the Jewish Fighting Organization and of the Secret Army, commanded by General Charles DE GAULLE, which participated in the liberation of southwestern France. About 150 members of Compagnie Marc Haguenau lost their lives fighting the Nazis.

After the Allies landed in Normandy in June 1944, La Sixième took an active role in the battle of liberation for France. It fought alongside the Allies until liberation and helped with anti-German sabotage, mostly on German armored trains.

EDELMAN, MAREK

(1921–) One of the commanders of the WARSAW GHETTO UPRISING. Edelman was born in Warsaw and was a member of Zukunft, the YOUTH MOVEMENT of the Jewish-Socialist Bund Party. During the Nazi occupation of POLAND (1939–1944), he became a leader

Marek Edelman

in the Warsaw ghetto UNDERGROUND and in the Bund's central administration. In November 1942, he joined the JEWISH FIGHTING ORGANIZATION (ZOB), and soon became a commander.

Edelman helped lead the Jewish RESISTANCE when German forces began to suppress the Warsaw Ghetto Uprising. The Nazis gradually destroyed the Warsaw ghetto and isolated the Jewish fighters. Edelman was one of a last group to hold out in the ZOB's headquarters at 18 Mila Street. He escaped on 10 May 1943, through the city's sewer network to the non-Jewish side of Warsaw.

In August 1944, Edelman and other Jewish members of the ZOB assisted in the general Polish uprising in Warsaw.

Edelman was one of the few survivors of the Warsaw Ghetto Uprising. He chose to remain in Poland after WORLD WAR II, and became a cardiologist. He was active in the Solidarity Movement led by Lech Walesa in the early 1980s.

EDELSTEIN, JACOB

(1903–1944) Head of the THERESIENSTADT ghetto. As the chief elder of its JUDENRAT, Jacob Edelstein was responsible for daily operations in the ghetto.

Edelstein was a Labor Zionist leader in CZECHOSLOVAKIA. Before WORLD WAR II, he rose through the ranks of the Labor Zionists and became the director of the PRAGUE office of the JEWISH AGENCY. Edelstein traveled extensively throughout Europe to evaluate the status of Jews in their home environments. Early in the war, he visited Jews at the NISKO AND LUBLIN detention reserve. He became convinced at that point that DEPORTATIONS almost certainly meant "death."

Edelstein called for the creation of a camp/reserve in the German Czech Protectorate in order to insure the safety of the Jews from BOHEMIA AND MORAVIA. The establishment of the Theresienstadt ghetto was partly due to his suggestion.

As the leader of the Judenrat, Edelstein is the subject of much controversy. On the one hand, some suggest that he collaborated with the Nazis, not realizing that Theresienstadt was only a temporary stop for most of the inmates who would be moved and killed. On the other hand, there are those who see him as a hero. He gave his life to save the lives of other Jews. Edelstein remained the

Jacob was in the same barracks as I was— number 13—on that Monday morning. It was about 9 a.m. and he was saying his morning prayers, wrapped in his prayer shawl. Suddenly the door burst open and SS Lieutenant Hoessler strutted in, accompanied by three SS men. He called out Jacob's name. Jacob did not move. Hoessler screamed: "I am waiting for you, hurry up."

Jacob turned round very slowly, faced Hoessler and said quietly, "Of the last moments on this earth, allotted to me by the Almighty, I am the master, not you." Whereupon he turned back to face the wall and finished his prayers. He then folded his prayer shawl unhurriedly, handed it to one of the inmates and said to Hoessler, "I am now ready."

Hoessler stood there all the while without uttering a word, and marched out when Edelstein was ready. Edelstein followed him and the three SS men made up the rear. We never saw Jacob Edelstein again.

Eye witness account of the last moments of Jacob Edelstein's life, by Yossl Rosensaft, a fellow inmate in Auschwitz

"Elder of the Jews"—the leader of the Judenrat—until late in 1943, when he, along with his family and three others, was arrested and deported to their deaths in AUSCHWITZ. The charge made against Edelstein was falsifying the census of Jews in the ghetto and enabling 55 ghetto residents to avoid deportation.

EICHMANN, ADOLF

(1906–1962) Nazi SS officer in charge of murdering the Jews of Europe.

Eichmann was born in Solingen, GERMANY, and spent his early childhood in Linz, Austria, a village not far from where Adolf HITLER spent his early years.

As a young adult, he took a job as a traveling salesman. During this period, he began to attend meetings of the Nationalist Socialists (Nazis), which stimulated his hatred of Jews. Eichmann believed

Jacob Edelstein (right) in Theresienstadt, watching the burial of ghetto inmates

that the Jews desired the destruction of Germany. In 1927, at the age of 21, he became a member of the Austro-German Veterans Organization, an extreme nationalist German group. In 1932, at age 26, he officially joined the Austrian Nazi party.

After Hitler's rise to power in 1933, Eichmann moved to Berlin, where he began his Nazi career as a file clerk. While at work, he heard of an opening in Heinrich HIMMLER'S SD, which was the intelligence branch of the GESTAPO.

Overestimating Eichmann's knowledge and understanding of Judaism and Hebrew, Himmler appointed him to the Jewish section of the SD. In this capacity, Eichmann made a short visit to PALESTINE in 1937. Upon his return to Germany, Eichmann quickly rose through the Nazi ranks. In 1938, he became the head of the Office of Jewish Emigration in AUSTRIA. The role of this office was to ease the bureaucracy that prevented Jews from leaving Austria and to encourage their voluntary emigration.

Because of its success, this example was followed elsewhere.

After 1939, Eichmann was appointed director of the Reich's Central Office of Jewish Emigration. In March 1941, he was promoted to lieutenant-colonel and made head of Subsection IV B-4 of the RSHA, the Reich Central Security Office in charge of the deportation of Jews (see REICHSSICHERHEITSHAUPTAMT). He remained in charge of executing every aspect of Nazi policies against the Jews until the end of the war.

Eichmann was present in January 1942, at the WANNSEE CONFERENCE, where the "FINAL SOLUTION" was determined. There plans were developed for deporting and exterminating the Jews of Europe. Eichmann was put in charge. He traveled all over Europe to ensure that the plan was fully carried out. So successful was this operation, according to Adolf Eichmann, that in August 1944 he reported to Himmler that although no exact statistics were available, 4 million Jews had already died in camps, and that 2 million more were shot by mobile killing units.

At the close of the war, Adolf Eichmann was arrested, but since his true identity was unknown, he was able to escape from an internment camp in the American sector. A massive manhunt began, lasting 15 years, for the man who had coordinated the murder machinery of the Nazis. On 11 May 1960, the Israeli secret service found Eichmann living in Argentina under a false name (Ricardo Klement). They kidnapped him and smuggled him to ISRAEL to stand trial for crimes against humanity, war crimes, and the murder of millions of Jews during the Holocaust.

Eichmann Trial On 23 May 1960, Israel's Prime Minister David BEN-GURION made a one-sentence statement to his parliament, saying that Adolf Eichmann was in Israel and would be brought to trial under the Nazis and Nazi Collaborators (Punishment) Law, which had been passed in 1950. Many months then passed while Eichmann was being interrogated, the indictment prepared and arrangements made for the trial. To Ben-Gurion the trial

served not only to bring to justice the man regarded as the main coordinator and often instigator of Hitler's "Final Solution" to the "Jewish Question" in Europe; but even more this was an opportunity to bring the Israeli public—especially the younger generation—to an awareness of the history and lessons of the Holocaust.

The trial opened in Jerusalem on 11 April 1961. A bench of three judges presided, headed by Judge Moshe Landau. The chief prosecutor was Israel's attorney general, Gideon Hausner; Eichmann was defended by a German lawyer, Dr. Robert Servatius, who had previously defended some of the Nazi leaders in the Nuremberg Trials of 1945–1946 (see TRIALS OF WAR CRIMINALS).

Hausner's opening speech, which lasted two days, summarized the events of the Holocaust, beginning: "When I stand here before you, judges of Israel, to lead the prosecution of Adolf Eichmann, I am not standing alone. With me are 6 million accusers. But they cannot rise to their feet and point an accusing finger, crying 'I accuse.' ...Their blood cries out but their voices are not heard." The prosecution brought 112 harrowing eyewitnesses to tes-

Adolf Eichmann, flanked by Israeli guards, at his trial in Jerusalem. In foreground the prosecuting lawyers (from right) Dr. Jacob Robinson, Gabriel Bach and Gideon Hausner. Standing, Eichmann's defending lawyer, Robert Servatius

tify about the history of the Holocaust and the experience of European Jewry in all countries concerned. One by one, witnesses told of the development of Nazi ANTISEMITISM, the anti-Jewish laws in country after country, the horror of the GHETTOS, the mass murders, and the DEATH CAMPS. K. Zetnik, writer and Auschwitz survivor, passed out on the stand. Deep emotions were stirred when one of the witnesses produced a child's pair of shoes that he had taken from TREBLINKA.

The courtroom was packed at every session. Many survivors attended, some becoming so carried away that they stood up and shouted. Eichmann, who, throughout the entire trial, stared fixedly ahead or at the judges. For his own protection, he sat in a bulletproof glass booth. The prosecution also brought 1,434 documents from German and other sources to demonstrate Eichmann's deep involvement and activities as head of the Gestapo's Jewish department, whose aim it had been to solve the "Jewish question."

The defense had few witnesses and most of these had been Nazis who would not come to Israel for fear of arrest. They were questioned in their own countries. Eichmann himself spent a month on the witness stand. The defense did not challenge the factual account of the events of the Holocaust or deny the authenticity of the documents produced. They insisted that Eichmann had not initiated anything but had only taken and obeyed orders, following his oath of loyalty to Hitler.

After four months, the defense and prosecution presented their summaries and the case was adjourned while the judges considered their verdict. They reassembled on 11 December 1961, and pronounced Eichmann guilty. Their verdict took four sessions to read and dealt thoroughly with all aspects of the case, ruling that Eichmann had stood at the head of the execution of the "Final Solution" and was responsible for all its phases. Indeed, his desire to destroy Jews became an obsession.

Eichmann was sentenced to death and the verdict was immediately appealed to the Supreme Court. A panel of five judges considered the appeal in March 1962, and confirmed the decision of the lower court, on 29 May 1962. After the president of Israel denied an appeal for clemency, Eichmann was hanged in Ramleh prison on 1 June. The body was

With a deep sense of the responsibility resting upon us, we have considered what is the proper penalty to be meted out to the accused, and have arrived at the conclusion that for the due punishment of the accused, and for the deterrence of others, the maximum penalty laid down by law has to be imposed in this case. We have described in our judgment the crimes in which the accused participated—crimes of unparalleled enormity in their nature and extent. The aim of the crimes against the Jewish people of which the accused has been convicted was to blot out an entire people from the face of the earth.

From the pronouncement of sentence
on Adolf Eichmann

To be frank with you, had we killed all of them, the 10.3 million, I would be happy and say, "all right, we managed to destroy an enemy."

From an interview with Eichmann,
conducted by Dutch Nazi journalist,
Willem Sassen, 1957

Eichmann was very cynical in his attitude to the Jewish question. He gave no indication of any human feeling toward these people. He was not immoral: he was amoral, and completely ice cold in his attitude.

Dieter Wisliceny, an associate of
Adolf Eichmann

Eichmann said, "I shall leap into my grave laughing because of the feeling that I have. The deaths of 5 million people on my conscience will be for me the source of extraordinary satisfaction."

Eichmann's last address to his men,
according to Dieter Wisliceny

cremated, and the ashes scattered at sea, beyond Israel's territorial waters. It was the only death sentence ever carried out in Israel.

The Eichmann trial achieved Ben-Gurion's main

goal—the creation of Holocaust awareness among younger Israelis, who had up to that time exhibited a coolness and lack of understanding. Many Holocaust SURVIVORS, who had kept their stories to themselves, now opened up and spoke of their experiences. The trial also had a widespread international impact. Covered by the world media on a daily basis, it promoted an awareness of the Holocaust. Its impact was particularly felt in Germany, where it stimulated the prosecution of war criminals.

The full transcript of the proceedings of the Eichmann Trial in English has been published in 9 volumes by the Israel Ministry of Justice, 1994–1995.

EICHMANN TRIAL

see EICHMANN, ADOLF.

EICKE, THEODOR

(1892–1943) SS Lieutenant General, Inspector of CONCENTRATION CAMPS and commander of the DEATH'S HEAD UNITS, an armed SS troop which guarded the camps. He began his career as a police officer after World War I. In 1928, he joined the NAZI PARTY and entered the SS in 1930. He had excellent relations with SS chief Heinrich HIMMLER. This allowed him to advance rapidly through the ranks of the SS, despite his often disagreeable personality. In June 1933, Eicke was named commandant of DACHAU the first Nazi concentration camp. His slogan was "Tolerance is a sign of weakness." His cruel leadership style at Dachau became a model for the growing Nazi camp system. By July 1934, Eicke had been promoted Inspector for Concentration Camps. He was also named commander of the SS Death's Head units Eicke earned this advancement as a reward for his involvement in the "Night of the Long Knives." This was a bloody purge of SA leaders carried out mainly by Himmler's SS. It was Eicke himself who shot SA chief Ernst RÖHM in his prison cell. The Death's Head units under Eicke became the core of the Death's Head Division of the Waffen SS, (militarized units of the SS). Eicke assumed the leadership of the Waffen SS in November 1939. Under his command, the division fought on both western and eastern fronts. Its reputation for brutality and its

Theodor Eicke

many war crimes convinced the victorious Allies to classify the Waffen SS as a "criminal organization" at the end of the war (see CRIMES AGAINST HUMANITY). Eicke died on 26 February 1943, when his plane was shot down on the Russian Front.

EINSATZGRUPPEN ("action-groups")

German term that was first used for Nazi police intelligence units working with the German army after the invasion of AUSTRIA, CZECHOSLOVAKIA and POLAND. These groups were disbanded at the end of 1939.

When GERMANY invaded SOVIET RUSSIA in June 1941, the term was applied to the mobile SS killing squads that traveled with the German forces. There were 3,000 to 4,000 men in the Einsatzgruppen, but they were assisted in their work by many COLLABORATORS from among the local populations of the occupied areas.

The special task of the Einsatzgruppen was to move from place to place and kill all Jews and suspected communists on the spot. Although this command was only issued orally, it was faithfully carried out. In a series of massacres, the Einsatzgruppen destroyed most of the Jewish population of the former Baltic States (LITHUANIA, LATVIA, ESTONIA), BYELORUSSIA (Belarus), and UKRAINE. The Einsatzgruppen were also responsible for forcing Jews into GHETTOS in those places that they were not killed immediately.

The Einsatzgruppen were divided into four groups: "A" (the largest) was assigned to Army Group North, and operated in the Baltic States; "B" was assigned to Army Group Central in Byelorussia and the territory to the east of Moscow; "C" was assigned to Army Group South in all but the southern part of Ukraine; and "D" (the smallest) was assigned to the 11th Army, which operated in the southern Ukraine and Crimea.

The worst period of these massacres was between June 1941 and early 1942 (Einsatzgruppe "D" alone reported over 165,000 victims in September 1941, and over 95,000 in October). The most common method of killing was by shooting. Jews were told they were going to be resettled and were ordered to assemble at a certain place. When gathered together, they were forced to hand their possessions over to the leaders of the unit. A short while before the murders, the victims would be ordered to remove all of their outer clothing (and sometimes undergarments as well). They were then led to a place of execution. This was often near a deep ditch, a shell crater or a pit—sometimes in the Jewish cemetery or in a forest. The victims would then be shot kneeling or standing and the corpses were tossed into the ditch. Executions were also carried out using the so-called "sardine method," in which the victims were made to lie down in the

A German soldier in an Einsatzgruppe takes aim at a Jewish mother and child while others prepare their grave during an aktion against the Jewish population of Ivangorod. This photo was enclosed in a letter of a German soldier on the eastern front to Germany. It was intercepted in the Warsaw post office by members of the Polish Home Army who kept surveillance over the mails. The German inscription on the back of the photo reads: "Ukraine 1942, Jewish Aktion, Ivangorod"

A mass execution by Einsatzgruppen in Kovno, Lithuania

bottom of the grave and shot. The next group of victims would then be forced to lie down with their heads to the victims' feet and this would be continued until the grave was full. The largest of these mass murders were those carried out in BABI YAR, near Kiev (Ukraine), and in PONARY, near Vilna (Lithuania).

The total number of victims of the Einsatzgruppen in the former Soviet Russia remains unknown. The number was certainly well over 1 million Jews, and hundreds of thousands of Russian civilians and prisoners of war. By 1942, the Germans had decided to begin killing Jews in GAS CHAMBERS at large, specially constructed DEATH CAMPS. This, and the fact that most Jews in the Einsatzgruppen area of operations had already been killed, led to the disbanding of these units.

Einsatzgruppen officers came from many different walks of life and included several lawyers, a Protestant pastor, a physician, an opera singer, and representatives of many other professions. All received special instruction in Nazi thought.

After the war, at a trial concluded in April 1948, 14 of 24 Einsatzgruppen members were sentenced to death. Only four were actually executed. One of the 14 sentenced to death and some of the others were released from prison as early as the mid-1950s.

Later, in West German trials, over 100 more charges were issued against Einsatzgruppen members, but none could be executed because West Germany had abolished the death sentence.

E I N S A T Z S T A B R O S E N B E R G

("Special Operations Staff Rosenberg")

An organization whose task was to seize valuable artistic and cultural objects from Jews. It was created by Alfred ROSENBERG in his capacity as head of the Center for National Socialist Ideological and Educational Research. The organization confiscated these objects in both eastern and western Europe on the grounds that they were "ownerless."

General Dwight D. Eisenhower (center) and a party of high ranking U.S. Army officers, including Generals Bradley, Patton, and Eddy, examine charred prisoners' remains on an inspection of the Ohrdruf concentration camp, Germany

Rosenberg was appointed head of the center by Adolf HITLER on 29 January 1940. In September 1940, Hitler created a Special Operations Staff for Fine Arts, and ordered it to seek out Jewish art treasures in newly-occupied FRANCE. This staff plundered famous art collections, such as that of the Rothschild family. It also searched for storehouses containing hidden works of art. In March 1942, Hitler confirmed Rosenberg's authority to seize cultural treasures and called on the German Army High Command to help him. Rosenberg's activities were now extended to all German-occupied countries.

In addition to the operations of the Staff for Fine Arts, an operation for the theft of furniture was conducted. At the Nuremberg TRIALS OF WAR CRIMINALS, it was estimated that this involved the looting of some 70,000 Jewish homes in western Europe, with 38,000 of them in PARIS alone. Rosenberg estimated that 40,000 tons of furniture had been brought to GERMANY to be given to Germans whose property had been damaged by bombing. Most of this came from the homes of Jews who had either been deported to their deaths or had managed to emigrate.

Rosenberg enjoyed the cooperation of the police in France and of local authorities in most western European countries. Operations in eastern Europe were not so well organized. Rosenberg's staff even faced competition there in plundering from organizations—such as a special "Battalion" for looting, set up by Joachim von RIBBENTROP. It will never be known exactly what was stolen in eastern Europe by these different groups. The scale of the thefts can be pictured from a letter written by Rosenberg's department. It claims that in October 1943 alone, 40 box-cars full of cultural and artistic treasures were moved from SOVIET RUSSIA to Germany.

EISENHOWER, DWIGHT D.

(1890–1969) Thirty-fourth president of the United States (1953–1961); supreme commander of the Allied troops in Europe in 1944; leader of the Allied landing in Normandy and of the campaign that led to the surrender of Nazi GERMANY. He was then appointed head of the occupation forces, leaving that post in 1948 to become president of Columbia University.

Eisenhower forced the French authorities to abolish the anti-Jewish laws of the VICHY government, and worked to cancel all Nazi racial and antisemitic laws once the Germans had surrendered. He commanded the troops who liberated tens of thousands of Jews from the CONCENTRATION CAMPS in Germany. When he visited the camps, he was deeply moved by what he saw and became convinced that such horrors should never happen again. He insisted on having as many American soldiers as possible visit the camps, so they could understand what had happened and bear witness. He spoke strongly about what he had seen at the camps on several occasions and wrote at length on the subject in his memoirs.

At his prompting, a special adviser on Jewish Affairs to the Supreme Commander of the Allied Forces was appointed to promote a solution to the plight of DISPLACED PERSONS (DPs). He arranged for separate camps to be set up for Jewish DPs in order to help them regain a sense of their Jewish identity. It was also General Eisenhower who gave the orders which led the army to turn a blind eye to the thousands of Jewish DPs from eastern Europe who were being smuggled into the American zone (see BERIHA). Following a meeting with David BEN-GURION in 1945, Eisenhower gave his permission for Hebrew teachers and agricultural instructors from PALESTINE to work in those camps, in order to prepare the DPs for emigration.

E N G L A N D

see GREAT BRITAIN.

E R N T E F E S T
(" H a r v e s t   F e s t i v a l ")

Code name for the operation to murder the last Jews of the TRAWNIKI and PONIATOWA LABOR CAMPS and the MAJDANEK DEATH CAMP. This operation took place on 3–5 November 1943. It was a response to Nazi fears of more uprisings following the revolt in the SOBIBÓR death camp on 14 October 1943.

Heinrich HIMMLER ordered the destruction of the remaining Jewish forced laborers who had been used by the SS within the GENERALGOUVERNEMENT. They numbered 40,000 to 43,000, 10,000 of whom were in Trawniki, 15,000 in Poniatowa, and 17,000 in Majdanek and its surrounding camps. Poniatowa and Trawniki were surrounded at dawn on 3 November. The Jews were marched out and shot by SS and police units. The bodies were thrown into specially prepared ditches. The Nazis had said these were anti-tank ditches to keep the plan a secret. Further secrecy was supplied by loud music, which was played to drown out the sound of the shooting. The remaining Jews from the FORCED LABOR camps around Majdanek were also brought there and shot. All the operations were carried out at the same time in order to surprise the victims and avoid resistance. Even so, the SS did encounter some resistance at Trawniki and Poniatowa, where the UNDERGROUND managed to set fire to some of the barracks.

Operation Erntefest was the final phase of AKTION REINHARD, the murder of the Jews of the Generalgouvernement.

ESCAPES FROM GHETTOS
A N D   C A M P S

After the walls went up around the GHETTOS, many people tried to get out. Some attempted to escape or to find hiding places. Others wanted to smuggle food and medicine back into the ghetto. It was also very important to get information both into and out of the ghetto. This was often done by young women who were fluent in the local language and customs. CHILDREN were also used to smuggle food into the ghetto, sometimes through sewers. RESISTANCE fighters also left the ghetto in order to strike at German targets and to receive military training.

Every ghetto had its weak points and its methods of escape. In a few, this was through the sewers. In others, it meant going over or through the surrounding wall or fence. In still other ghettos, escapees would slip out of formation while on work detail. Many of the escapes ended in tragedy. Some people got lost in the sewers. Others were captured or shot by the Nazis while trying to get out.

In VILNA, Abba KOVNER and others took most of the resistance fighters out of the ghetto to join the

Exit of sewage tunnel under Kraków, Poland, used for escaping from the ghetto

PARTISAN fighters. In KRAKÓW, Jewish fighters would leave the ghetto to strike at Nazi targets and then return, so as not to place the ghetto population at risk for Nazi revenge.

Escape was nearly impossible from the CAMPS. The prisoners' physical condition was so poor that escape was hard to imagine. Most of the prisoners did not know the geographic location of their camps. Even if they were able to attempt an escape, they would have no idea in which direction to turn to find refuge.

Despite this, mass breakouts took place in TREBLINKA and in SOBIBÓR. Of the several hundred who broke out in each case, most were caught within a few hours, and by the end of the day, nearly everyone who had escaped was shot.

In AUSCHWITZ, 667 prisoners escaped, 270 of whom were caught, interrogated, and then murdered. Most escapes from Auschwitz came about when a prisoner was moved into a more privileged position, especially as a worker in the hospital or as a secretary within the camp administration. As of 1943, these jobs became available to JEWS. Seventy-six escapes followed. Only a handful succeeded in getting beyond a small distance from the camp.

People usually attempted to escape to save their lives, but some wanted to inform the world about what was happening in the camps.

E S T O N I A

Country on the Baltic Sea. Prior to the Holocaust, about 4,500 Jews lived there.

In 1940, Estonia was forcibly annexed to SOVIET RUSSIA. Shortly after, all Jewish organizations and institutions were banned. About 500 of the communal leaders and the wealthy were arrested and deported to LABOR CAMPS in Russia.

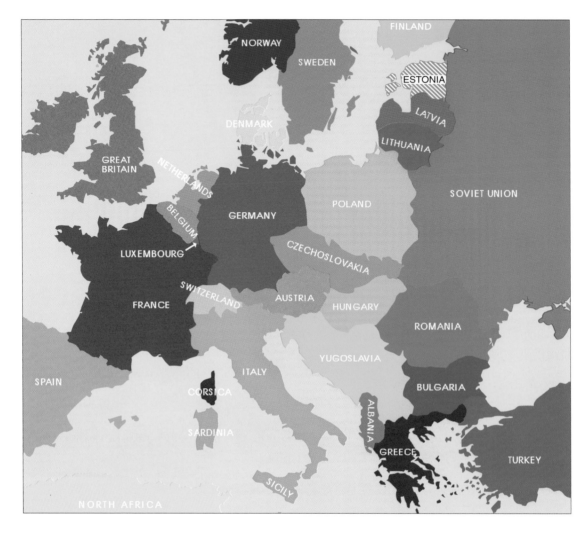

In the time between the German invasion of the Soviet Union in June 1941 and the actual occupation of Estonia in September 1941, about 3,000 Jews had fled from Estonia to the interior of the Soviet Union. Those that remained were murdered by the EINSATZGRUPPEN with the assistance of Estonians. Estonians served as volunteers in the SS and worked in a number of CONCENTRATION CAMPS as guards. At the Nazi WANNSEE CONFERENCE, early in 1942, Estonia was the only European country described as *Judenfrei* ("free of Jews").

However, in 1942–1943, several thousand Jews from GERMANY and elsewhere were deported to FORCED LABOR camps in Estonia. When the Red Army approached Estonia, these camps were closed and most of the survivors were forced on DEATH MARCHES. Others were killed on the spot, including about 2,400 at the camp at Klooga.

E U G E N I C S

The science that attempts to improve the traits that people inherit. Its aim is to perfect future generations by discouraging unfit characteristics while encouraging the most fit and desirable traits. The problem arises in determining what is desirable and fit and what is not. A doctrine of racial eugenics had developed already before World War I.

According to the German racial doctrine, ARYANS were supposed to exemplify the highest quality of the German race. The objective was to weed out the weakest people and those who "contaminate" society, while encouraging the best and the strongest to have many children. In July 1933, the Nazi Law for the Protection of Hereditary Health was passed for the purpose of eliminating all potential "infection" of the "pure" German race. This led to the so-called EUTHANASIA (mercy) killings of the physically and mentally handicapped who were, by this definition, suffering from incurable ailments. This policy was called Aktion T4, code-named after HITLER's Chancellory address, at Tiergartenstrasse 4.

The Nazis attempted to prove their superiority through eye and hair color, head shape, forehead angle and nose size and alignment. These pseudo-scientists developed charts and diagrams to prove their point and to instruct the German public in easy identification of valued ARYAN traits. In so doing, the ulterior motive of the German leadership was to prove the inferiority of others, especially Jews, thereby making it easier to exterminate them as they would any lesser creatures such as insects, vermin and rodents.

E U R O P A   P L A N

An attempt to save an estimated 1 million Jews from extermination, initiated in the summer of 1942 by the WORKING GROUP of Bratislava.

At the suggestion of the group, Dieter WISLICENY, Adolf EICHMANN's emissary to SLOVAKIA, was approached. He agreed to serve as a mediator in negotiations with the SS. The plan involved paying a large ransom in exchange for halting the DEPORTATION of Slovakian JEWS. As negotiations continued, the scope of the plan grew to include the remainder of European Jewry. The amounts involved included 40,000 to 50,000 dollars to Wisliceny, with 2 to 3 million U.S. dollars as the total ransom. Jewish organizations, mainly the AMERICAN JEWISH JOINT DISTRIBUTION COMMITTEE (JDC), were expected to pay the amounts.

Wisliceny did receive an advance payment of $20,000, which apparently was sent to the SS. The deportations stopped at that time, although it has never been proved that Wisliceny's intervention was the cause. Nevertheless, the Working Group took this as encouragement to proceed. The negotiations broke off at Heinrich HIMMLER's order and the Europa Plan was abandoned. Members of the group remained convinced that the reason for failure was that the money did not come from Jewish organizations. Yet evidence shows that the JDC representative in Geneva had been willing to deposit the money in special accounts in Switzerland, to be released after the war. Others have suggested that the

SS never really intended to make a deal, and that the Nazi "willingness" to negotiate was really counter-propaganda.

EUTHANASIA PROGRAM

Widespread so-called "mercy killings," code-named T4, performed by Nazi doctors on the mentally handicapped, mentally ill, the infirm, the aged and habitual criminals, to name a few. The belief that extraordinary measures should be taken to ensure the purity of the master race (HERRENVOLK) was central to the Nazi ideology. Those of lesser racial types were a threat to ARYANISM, a threat that had to be destroyed. A program of forced sterilization had already been in force for most of the 1930s, with the number of victims mounting to 350,000. In the late fall of 1939, HITLER named Philippe Bouhler and Dr. Karl BRANDT to head up a large scale euthanasia action. This would result in the deaths of hundreds of thousands.

Four centers were established in GERMANY (Grafeneck, Brandenburg, Hartheim and Sonnenstein) within the first six months of 1940. Victims were gassed, shot, or killed by lethal injection. By the end of 1940, nearly 27,000 people had been put to death in this program. By the end of 1941, the figure had reached 93,521. Public criticism of the Euthanasia Program forced its official closure on 1 September 1941, but it still continued. The widespread use of euthanasia as part of the Nazi obsession with racial purity persisted up until the end of the war and spread to the Nazi-occupied areas as well.

Two aspects of the Euthanasia program demand attention. First, the individuals who actually admin-

> *When asked "Have you, as a doctor, no respect for human life?", SS doctor, Fritz Klein responded: "Out of respect for human life, I would remove a purulent appendix from a diseased body. The Jew is the purulent appendix of the body of Europe."*
>
> *from Prisoners of Fear,*
> *Ella Lingens-Reiner (London: 1948)*

On the way to a Euthanasia center in Austria

istered the euthanasia were medical personnel. Dr. Brandt's staff were doctors by training. The people involved in the medical experiments taking place in the CONCENTRATION CAMPS and in the selections in which arriving prisoners were sent to their deaths were members of the health care professions. Second, the victims of the Euthanasia Program were largely German citizens with families, but resistance by the families and by the churches was extremely limited. Of course, there was sufficient protest against the program to force it under cover. Some clergymen, particularly Bishop Ludwig Sebastian in August of 1942, used their pulpits to speak out against the program. This was after the program had already claimed 100,000 German citizens as its victims. It would therefore seem that public support for the larger concern of creating a "master race" overcame the revulsion some might have felt for disposing of " inferior" individuals, even among fellow citizens and family members.

According to testimony heard at the Nuremberg TRIALS, the total number of victims of the Euthanasia Program approached 275,000. This figure includes the aged, HOMOSEXUALS, residents of welfare institutions, concentration camp inmates and, toward the end of the war, even sick German soldiers.

EVIAN CONFERENCE

International meeting convened by U.S. President Franklin D. ROOSEVELT in July 1938 at Evian, FRANCE, in face of the growing refugee problem. Following the rise of Nazism in GERMANY and AUSTRIA after the

ANSCHLUSS, the conference's stated goal was to find new havens for "political and racial" refugees. No official mention was made of the fact that most of the refugees were JEWS, although that reality was understood by all at the conference. In addition, President Roosevelt declared in the invitation to the conference that no country would be forced to change its immigration laws or quotas; instead, each country was asked to consider voluntary changes in immigration policy.

As the conference proceeded it became evident that little would be accomplished. Representative after representative declared that his own country was filled with refugees and could admit no more. Jewish representatives attempted to sway the conference on humanitarian grounds, but failed to do so. In particular, representatives of the JEWISH AGENCY and the WORLD JEWISH CONGRESS tried to convince the conference of the need to keep PALESTINE (Israel) open for Jewish refugees. The Zionists hoped to bring international pressure to bear on the British government. They wanted GREAT BRITAIN to grant enlarged immigration schedules and reverse the increasing restrictions on Jewish immigration that had begun in 1937. Only one country, the Dominican Republic, made any offer to accept refugees, and even that offer was contingent upon massive payments to the Dominican government by the AMERICAN JEWISH JOINT DISTRIBUTION COMMITTEE. The conference failed in its stated goal and had only one

Myron C. Taylor of the U.S., closing the intergovernmental meeting at Evian on political refugees, over which he presided.

concrete result, of questionable value: the creation of an Intergovernmental Committee on Refugees.

"EXODUS 1947"

Ship that attempted to bring 4,500 Jewish survivors to PALESTINE in the summer of 1947, despite the fact that Jewish immigration to PALESTINE (Israel) was severely restricted by the British at that time.

In July 1947, the JEWISH AGENCY's secret service, the Mossad, which was working to bring Jews to Palestine, planned its most ambitious operation. A river excursion boat, the *President Warfield*, was renamed *Exodus 1947*. It was loaded with 4,500 HOLOCAUST survivors who had been living in German refugee camps, and set sail from Marseilles, FRANCE. The *Exodus 1947* was captured by the British after a brief fight, in which many were injured. Three of the would-be immigrants were killed. The British took the ship to the port of Haifa in Palestine. There they transferred all the passengers to three deportation ships. Despite their protests and protests from around the world, the ships were ordered to return to France. The French refused to allow the passengers to land and, after standing offshore for three months, the British decided to send the ships to GERMANY and unload the passengers there, by force. This decision was carried out with full media coverage on 8 September 1947.

The *Exodus* affair had a major impact on world public opinion bringing support for the Zionist struggle to establish a Jewish State. The unfortunate *Exodus* passengers remained in German refugee camps until 1948, when they were finally able to depart for the State of Israel.

This story was the basis of a popular book in the 1950s by Leon Uris, called *Exodus*, which was also made into a successful film of the same title.

EXTERMINATION CAMPS

see DEATH CAMPS.

British soldiers in Haifa forcing refugees to get off the "Exodus 1947" in order to transfer them to other boats for deportation to France where they were forced to remain on board for three months and then taken to Germany

index

Bold numbers indicate an entry on the subject in this volume. See volume 4 for a full set index.